THE MADISON EFFECT

AN INSPIRING CULTURE OF CALL

Thank you for answering God's call!!
Gary Robbins

GARY ROBBINS

ISBN 978-1-64471-227-6 (Paperback)
ISBN 978-1-64471-228-3 (Digital)

Copyright © 2019 Gary Robbins
All rights reserved
First Edition

All rights reserved. No part of this publication may be reproduced, distributed, or transmitted in any form or by any means, including photocopying, recording, or other electronic or mechanical methods without the prior written permission of the publisher. For permission requests, solicit the publisher via the address below.

Covenant Books, Inc.
11661 Hwy 707
Murrells Inlet, SC 29576
www.covenantbooks.com

To those who answered Isaiah's call to stand behind a pulpit each week, and to the volunteers who leave the walls of the church to care for others

Contents

Acknowledgments 7

Introduction 9

Chapter 1: The Madison Effect: A Culture of Call 15

Chapter 2: Whom Shall I Send? (Isaiah 6:8) 23

Chapter 3: Great Unrealistic Expectations 34

Chapter 4: Effective Ministry Partnerships 49

Chapter 5: Here I Am, Send Me (Isaiah 6:8) 59

Chapter 6: What Is Your Spiritual Footprint? 76

"Just finished reading and being inspired yet again with the Madison Effect. Seeing the book as a whole is nothing short of amazing. I do believe that God inspired you as you wrote. This book will be a good resource for local churches and congregations."

—Rev. Linda Louderback

"The Madison Effect is such a powerful and inspiring book. It is exactly what is needed. I love the book. I hope seminaries put it at the top of required reading. Church leaders serving with clergy should read it before taking leadership positions. God will use this to strengthen the Church in many places. Great Work!"

—Rev. Larry Fry

Acknowledgments

I am indebted to the clergy and laity who generously shared their time and life lessons to make this book a reality. I owe my deepest thanks to my wife, Donna, for her patience and assistance in preparation of the book. Rev. Linda Louderback challenged me to explore further and provided invaluable assistance in editing this book. Finally, I owe so much to my Countryside church family for their amazing influence and insights on my faith journey.

Introduction

While attending a Methodist Youth Fellowship meeting when I was in the seventh grade, I was talking and fooling around when I should have been listening and paying attention. I have always wondered if the Holy Spirit dropped the twelve-inch glass cover from the light fixture directly above me. The timing was impeccable and generated hysterical laughter when it hit my head. The laughter lasted until we had to clean up hundreds of shards of glass. (Sadly, my behavior still mirrors a seventh grader too often!) It did get my attention, and the Holy Spirit still redirects me as needed. Coincidentally, the idea for this book hit me like a plummeting light fixture. Forty years as a church volunteer has bombarded me with ideas and stories that needed to be shared. I began gathering each piece of these inspirational stories like the many shards of glass that fell on me so long ago. It starts with a visit to a remarkable church.

The small, rural United Methodist Church in Madison, Kansas, has an extraordinary culture of call that has sent sixteen members into ministry. It is what I call the Madison Effect. The Madison Effect described in the first chapter is urgently needed in churches and denominations to address the need for more clergy. This book is written from the perspective of a layperson who has been blessed with some amazing learning opportunities. I have four decades of experience working with volunteers in nonprofit associations, serving as a volunteer in my own congregation and serving on four different boards with clergy and other laypersons from across Kansas and Nebraska. Unfortunately, in the Great Plains United Methodist Church Conference covering Kansas and Nebraska, we see more pastors retiring than entering the ministry. While the context of this book is the United Methodist Church (UMC), there is an urgent need for pastors and ministry volunteers that applies to all churches.

"Whom shall I send?" is the challenging question posed in the book of Isaiah in chapter 6:8. I am blessed to be a witness to those who responded in Kansas and Nebraska. In the spring of each year the lay members of the Great Plains Board of Ordained Ministry have the privilege of joining the clergy gathering during the Great Plains UMC Annual conference. We hand out materials and assist with the logistics as seven hundred to eight hundred ministers enter the meeting hall. It is overwhelming to see the hands and feet of Jesus Christ in these pastors who serve more than a thousand communities in every corner of Kansas and Nebraska. They are a diverse group, ranging from those nearing retirement to those who appear to be in high school. The sense of community, with laughter and the joy of seeing old friends, colleagues, or classmates, is accompanied by a buzz of excitement and crowd noise that is joyful to the Lord. It is exciting to see the energy entering the meeting hall. Serving in this unique position allows the board members to see the professional growth, the hard work, and sacrifice paving the way for the privilege of entering the meeting hall. I always shed a tear of joy when I look around the room and give thanks to God for their willingness to answer Isaiah's call.

I have enjoyed participating and teaching part-time in a Sunday morning Bible study for more than twenty years. Three class members went on to seminary. It was amazing to watch the dynamic power of this small group as they continued their spiritual journey and entered the ministry.

The second chapter illustrates the importance of congregational discernment for the Madison Effect to work in identifying future leaders willing to answer Isaiah's call. The chapter explores five different call stories from Kansas and Nebraska clergy. Often, the Holy Spirit is assisted by discerning pastors and "persistently invitational" laypersons who identify and mentor those who have the gifts for ministry.

Congregational discernment and accountability requires a thorough understanding of the "Art of Pew Sitting" needed to make disciples for Jesus Christ. The third chapter addresses four aspects of pew sitting: eliminating unrealistic expectations from the pews; avoiding passive pew sitting; becoming more invitational; and, finally, avoiding my "pew pet peeves." The book challenges the reader to imagine standing behind a pulpit to eliminate unrealistic expectations for pastors. While giving updates on the value of attending a Christian liberal arts college, I survived two traumatic "pulpit experiences." Both gave me a deep appreciation for those standing behind the pulpit each Sunday.

Elimination of apathy and inaction caused by passive pew sitting is vital! Passive pew sitters range from people who seldom come to worship to those who regularly attend and are growing in their faith but haven't left their pew to serve. To address this issue, we need to ask how the Madison Church inspired so many members into ministry and mission. The giving of our time, talents, and resources will increase the effectiveness of your pastor and ministry of the local congregation. I have created and will use in this book the term *pewster*. It is a joyful derivation of the words *pew* and *minister*. It designates congregation members who are actively involved in their own personal spiritual growth through the study of the scriptures, commitment to making disciples for Jesus Christ, and the realization that sitting in the pew causes them to go beyond the walls of our churches to serve others. I *will explore the Madison Effect and how it create*s *a culture of call that is designed to inspire ministry volunteers and passionate* pewsters. Both are essential to provide ministry and future volunteer leadership for our churches.

Of course, this book will address some of the delicate aspects of pew etiquette. Why are you sitting in my pew? Haven't I seen you here before? Why isn't the sermon entertaining me? We have always done it that way! I have been guilty of some of these transgressions; therefore, I am a self-proclaimed expert as a recovering passive pew sitter. I am still researching the ongoing question of why people want to sit in the front of the plane, middle of the road, and back of the church. I will incorporate my general observations from interviews with candidates for ordination to examine what constitutes clergy-friendly churches.

To appropriately nurture our clergy, we must ask some tough questions. Why don't we always show appropriate esteem and respect for clergy engaged in the life-changing work they perform each week? We too often take pastors for granted. Generally, they are underpaid, underappreciated, unfairly critiqued, and not always appropriately supported by their congregations. Hundreds of thousands of ministers, priests, and pastors take to the pulpit each Sunday, and, in many cases, the only times the clergy are recognized are when someone retires, gets into trouble, or it happens to be Clergy Appreciation Sunday.

The fourth chapter discusses how we nurture our pastors and create positive partnerships for ministry through the vital role of Staff Parish Relations Committees or personnel committee of the church. This requires effective communication between pastors and congregations. Sometimes congregations don't realize their essential role in the spiritual care and nurturing of clergy, which is essential for the development of future church leaders from within our congregations. Effective clergy-congregation partnerships create clergy-friendly churches.

The fifth chapter explores the unlimited opportunities to serve as volunteers for church ministries, nonprofit service agencies, and other mission opportunities at home and abroad. We will meet some of the amazing church leaders who touched my life. The chapter is entitled "Here I Am, Send Me," which reflects on responding to the call presented to each of us in Isaiah 6:8. There will always be tasks that allow the young and more mature volunteers to serve. There are devoted Christians providing ministry to us from coffee shops, nursing homes, and other diverse settings. The care and support of our church volunteers is an essential aspect of congregational awareness and maintaining a culture of call for volunteering. I will share my six lessons to identify volunteers and nurture them. In order to assure a flourishing culture of call for volunteering, I include recommendations on how to avoid burning out volunteers.

More than forty years of service to professional nonprofit associations and working alongside dedicated volunteers has provided many lessons to share that may also apply to churches. I had the privilege of representing the Kansas Optometric Association advocating for optometrists and their patients for more than three decades.

They inspired me and taught me so much about volunteering. They showed patience and grace when I made mistakes, which needs to be offered regularly to our pastors and church volunteers. The optometrists were often active in their churches, synagogues, and communities on top of their amazing charity work and leadership in worldwide mission efforts. I have served on four United Methodist conference-level boards and have learned so much by interacting with clergy and other pew sitters. I have always enjoyed the joke "The good Lord didn't create anything without a purpose, but mosquitoes and church meetings come close." I seem to recall that both Jesus and Moses had some challenging church meetings. The insights from the boardroom will be useful in our efforts toward understanding congregational excellence and a culture of volunteering.

I am sharing the lessons I have learned as a volunteer with congregations in order to help create a deeper appreciation for their essential role in effective partnerships with their pastors. The opportunity to interview and listen to those seeking to become ordained pastors in the Great Plains United Methodist Church as they serve their first churches has been an eye-opening experience. It has been through them that we see the good, the complacent, and, occasionally, the turmoil within congregations. There are simply some comments that pastors can't say to congregations and which need to be addressed by laity. This book is a challenge for congregations to reexamine how they nurture the clergy sent to serve them, practice a culture of call, mentor church volunteers, eliminate passive pew sitting, and build effective ministry partnerships with clergy.

The Madison Effect: An Inspiring Culture of Call concludes by examining and imagining the spiritual footprint that can be left by any church. Are we trying to leave a larger spiritual footprint in our churches, our communities, and the world each day? Are we trying to measure or discern how well we are doing in making disciples for Jesus Christ? The questions posed are designed to provide tools for a healthy congregational evaluation and discernment for churches as John Wesley would expect. My prayer is this book will help individual churches find a road map with workable answers and solutions in their own church settings.

Chapter 1

The Madison Effect: A Culture of Call

On a beautiful autumn day in October, I had the opportunity to travel through the scenic Flint Hills to the Madison United Methodist Church (UMC) in Madison, Kansas. It is just south of Emporia, Kansas. The small town of less than a thousand is nestled in a beautiful valley in Greenwood County. Pastor Laura Burnett had graciously agreed to open the church. She gave me a tour, and we talked about ministry in a smaller church with its unique challenges and opportunities. The church was charming and a sacred site of inspiration for me. I came to look at sixteen pictures hung in the back of the sanctuary which represent a culture of the call to ministry. I was impressed by the discipleship, dynamic ministry, and innovation I saw in this small church.

Why make the pilgrimage to Madison? A decade before, I had served on the Board of Discipleship for the Kansas East Conference of the United Methodist Church. The board was staffed by Reverend Gary Beach, the conference treasurer. The ministers and lay members I met while serving on the board inspired me to learn more about discipleship. In his ministry, Reverend Beach had served in the role of a district superintendent supervising more than sixty churches, including the Madison United Methodist Church. Rev. Beach told a story about one rural church that had sent sixteen members into the ministry. It was the Madison UMC. This book could not be written without a pilgrimage to see the church along with an attempt to understand how they created and maintained a culture of call to ministry among their members for almost a century.

There were fourteen pictures of ministers and two missionaries to South America hanging on the back wall of the sanctuary. I stood on a chair to take several down and dust them off. I was a little disappointed that there were only names and no dates of when these individuals entered the ministry. Based on the attire, I would estimate that the first ministers were in the late 1930s, but it is only a guess. I was elated to see the picture of Larry Fry as the sixteenth member to enter the ministry. Early in his ministry, Larry had served as our associate minister at Countryside United Methodist Church in Topeka, Kansas, where I attend.

Since my research started with the Madison United Methodist Church pictures, I decided to interview Rev. Larry Fry, recently retired, to learn more about the Madison UMC. I was anxious to seek his insights after forty years of ministry and learn more about the Madison Effect.

After leaving the Madison UMC, I asked myself a series of questions on the drive home. Imagine the impact left by this small church and those touched by fourteen ministers and two missionaries! It is overwhelming to comprehend. Reverend Beach told me that Madison UMC was disappointed that another youth from their community hadn't entered the ministry in the last decade. They still expect that members consider entering the ministry even though the last one retired from ministry in 2015 after more than forty years in the pulpit. I recently looked at the website, and the church photo showed their message board outside the church for that week. It said, "If you are going to sleep in on Sunday, please do it here." I love their witty invitational spirit.

This is an impressive culture of call spanning two centuries. The Madison UMC was founded in 1921 and is approaching its centennial. How many lives did this small, rural church touch, and how many seeds did they plant in South America and the United States? How many disciples for Jesus Christ did they make? Next, I wondered how many hospital visits, baptisms, weddings, and funerals they performed while providing pastoral care. How many folks did they lead to Jesus Christ? How many other Christians did they inspire to become church leaders or enter the ministry and are serving congregations today? Finally, the big question… *What is the lasting spiritual footprint of the Madison Effect?*

The power of the Gospel and the Holy Spirit uses churches and pastors committed to seeking those with the gifts for ministry to make the Madison Effect a reality and bear fruit. I am sure there are many other churches in all types of settings striving to make the Madison Effect a reality. My home church, Countryside UMC, is only sixty-five years old and currently has around 1,200 members with five hundred to six hundred in worship. We have sent only seven members into the ministry. This includes two members finishing seminary. We are significantly larger than the Madison UMC, yet not even half as successful as this small church in Greenwood County. The importance of a culture of call is needed, with looming shortages of ministers, pastors, and priests in some denominations. Some churches may have forgotten that creating a culture of call was one of their responsibilities. More churches are starting to address and affirm the responsibility to identify and nurture future leaders.

When I initially spoke with Reverend Fry, he pointed out that he was the third pastor from the Madison church to serve Countryside United Methodist Church. I was stunned that the Madison UMC had sent pastors to help lead us for more than sixty years. The other Madison pastors who served Countryside UMC were Neil Heidrick and John Richter. I had no idea. This provided me with a dramatic example of the spiritual footprint of Madison UMC.

Rev. Larry Fry recalled one minister named Rev. Arthur Hardy, who made sure that the Madison UMC youth were given opportunities to attend church camps and missions. If someone couldn't afford it, he helped or found someone to pay the cost. If parents couldn't drive, either he did it himself or found someone who would. This is a trait of a pastor that churches often take for granted. As a youth, Larry was a camp counselor and helped lead mission trips to develop his leadership skills. These experiences awakened and confirmed his personal call to ministry. I asked Larry to share his call story. It shows the spiritual footprint left by his United Methodist pastors and a committed, loving congregation like the Madison UMC.

Reverend Larry Fry's Call Story

My dad got a teaching job in Madison, Kansas, when I was five. We lived halfway between grandparents in Emporia and Hamilton, Kansas. Mom and Dad became involved in the Madison UMC, a very active and vital faith community during the '50s and '60s. Church school, a junior choir, youth group, adult choir, dinners, picnics, and worship—all included fun, fellowship, and encouragement. The church seemed more willing to emphasize the teachings and actions of Jesus than to argue about doctrine. The pastors made an impact, but the lay disciples made the biggest influence. Except for a few who tried to strangle the joy and life out of the Gospel. I felt valued and included by adult leaders and teachers; *participation* was always valued more highly than *perfection*. At age six, I turned my poster over during a Christmas pageant finale, not knowing it faced the congregation upside down. At age twelve, I was asked to read the Christmas story. I had no idea what *espoused* meant so I read it as Joseph and his *exposed* wife, Mary. Through my loving parents and the Madison church, I began to feel "caught" by something (the Holy Spirit), an amazing life-giving and life-changing force for good. Amazing lay and clergy leaders at camps, Baldwin Institute, and the United Nations DC Tour strengthened my faith in Christ and expanded my horizons of possibilities for my involvement in the church as a leader. Rev. Ray

Firestone invited me to serve as a summer youth intern at Parsons, Kansas, and other invitations followed. My growing inner call to the ministry was affirmed by positive responses from the Annual Conference and from those I served. The School of Religion at KU (University of Kansas) was a powerful influence, and I was off to Boston University School of Theology. During that time, Penny and I were married, and she joined me as I served a church in Lunenburg, Massachusetts, and then in a United Church of Christ house church in Fitchburg. I am in awe of her loving support as she pursued her career in social work.

Seminary was an amazing experience of spiritual growth; my goal to serve local churches led to a greater emphasis in the field of education and leadership. We returned to Kansas. I was privileged to serve United Methodist Churches at Beattie-Oketo, Berryton, Topeka Countryside, Meriden-Ozawkie, and Manhattan College Avenue. What started as imitating my parents became something more important. Yes, God might work through me and others teaming together. I am grateful for every part of God's call and for forty-four years of serving as a pastor. As one seminary student said, "The church is starving, locked in a grocery store, arguing about labels." I am grateful the Holy Spirit is working to change this through a new emphasis on witness (deed and word) and the call.

Reverend Fry's spiritual footprint, even though subjective and difficult to measure, is worthy of closer examination. I hope you feel challenged and inspired to start thinking about how your church can leave a larger spiritual footprint in the lives of others.

Larry's reference to church camps reminds me of a recent story in which ministers were needed to help with a session of a youth church camp. When one minister stepped up and volunteered to serve, he found that his own church considered it as "time off" and he had to use vacation time to be a church camp counselor. Spending a week at church camp with junior high students deserves a medal of valor and a pay raise. I am just kidding, but you get my point. I am disappointed when I hear stories about churches behaving inappropriately and not helping foster a culture of call. I can't think of a better use of time for a pastor than helping shape the spiritual lives of youth attending a church camp, mission trip, or youth institute! My point is that preachers are often the ones that spark the fire for someone to explore whether they are called to the ministry. Reverend Fry's call story strongly illustrates this point.

Reverend Fry mentioned another story about effective partnerships during a pastoral transition to a new church. On his first Sunday, there was a standoffish gentleman in the corner with a critical eye who finally came over and introduced himself. He said, "I am going to be watching you." Larry's first impression was that this was another habitual critic. But then this man spoke words of encouragement and hope that any newly appointed minister would want to hear. "I will do whatever I can to help you and our church, so we can do what God wants." Positive words of laity from the pews is essential for effective ministry partnerships to make disciples for Jesus Christ. Reverend Fry used the term "lay disciples," which perfectly defines a pewster.

Larry believes that churches need to be asking, "What is God wanting to do through us?" If everyone is connected and growing in spirit and expanding the mission of the church, amazing and powerful ministry can be accomplished. Before Larry arrived at College Avenue UMC in Manhattan, Kansas, the church had adopted six guiding values for their ministry. When disagreements and disputes occurred about ministry, they check to see if the item under discussion fit within the guiding principles. The guiding values were compassion, dignity, hospitality, spiritual growth, community, and discipleship. This approach helped resolve potentially divisive issues without causing deep divisions. When a potential opportunity for a new ministry or even a disagreement arose, they consulted the six guiding principles. Other churches may use their mission statement for this purpose. Coincidentally, our current Countryside UMC Pastor of Congregational Care, Rev. Nancy Gammill, was the pastor who helped College Avenue Church develop those guiding principles.

Every church should be asking if they are creating a culture of call to ministry and to mission within the church. The size of the church certainly doesn't matter, but clearly smaller churches like the Madison church are often the leaders and vital incubators for training aspiring pastors and sending members into the ministry. In some cases, those churches were rewarded when that individual previously in the pews of their church ended up behind the pulpit as their local pastor or certified lay minister. They may even inspire someone who will be your pastor in the future. We must nurture and support our pastors and each other to make disciples for Jesus Christ. My goal would be for churches to be asking the question posed by Reverend Fry: "What is God wanting to do through us?" Is it worth the effort to raise funds for youth to attend a spiritual retreat or camp? Is it worth your time to encourage someone and point out that they have the gifts for ministry? Often those individuals may be sitting next to you in a small group, Bible study, or in your pew. A culture of call can't exist without a concerted effort, watchful eyes, discerning ears, and constant prayer by the congregation. Pastors offer inspiration from the pulpit, but others are called to see the spiritual gifts in others first and start praying for them and encouraging them to consider the ministry.

Discernment Questions

- How is your church promoting a culture of call? In your discussion, use the examples learned from the Madison United Methodist Church. How did they develop expectations for members entering the mission field, entering the ministry, and becoming ministry volunteers? Consider small groups, your current congregational leadership, your

mission or vision statement, and other ministry projects to get a complete look at what you already have in place.
- Once you have completed your church assessment, consider the question posed by Fry, "What is God wanting to do through us?" Can some of these areas be strengthened? Are some ministries no longer viable or need revitalization? What new opportunities might be added to meet Fry's challenge?
- Recall the seminary student who said, "The church is starving, locked in a grocery store, arguing about labels." What does this mean, and is this a challenge for your church?

Chapter 2

Whom Shall I Send?
(Isaiah 6:8)

I want to clarify my definition of a "culture of call." It is an awareness and ongoing effort to help and encourage students, laity, or pewsters to identify their potential gifts for ministry as a pastor or a church leader. In the first chapter, I illustrated the power of the Madison Effect generated by just one small rural church sending sixteen members into ministry. What could hundreds or thousands of churches with an ongoing emphasis on a culture of call in their mission statement accomplish? It is exciting to prayerfully imagine.

Simply exploring the process of attending seminary can also create future church lay leaders, pewsters (lay disciples), and new pastors. Today there are many exciting possibilities in the United Methodist Church and other churches to become a certified lay minister or lay speaker (lay servants). Technology provides us with exciting new ways to learn, start seminary, and reinforce a culture of call. Annually, the Great Plains Board of Ordained Ministry hears the call stories from candidates seeking to become ordained ministers in the United Methodist Church. A few are dramatic experiences, but most involve a gradual process of discernment with spiritual growth and always include the work of the Holy Spirit.

Let me give a personal illustration of how spiritual gifts and the potential for ministry become apparent during small groups, Bible study, and mission projects. More than twenty-five years ago, we had an associate pastor named Edith Funk who started an adult Sunday school class designed to read the entire Bible in three years. It turned out to be a seven-year journey, but it was a joy! Let's just say we were not overachievers nor valedictorians of our high school graduating classes. There were survivors, but the associate minister wasn't one of them, as Rev. Edith Funk left for another appointment. The class stayed together studying the Bible an additional decade with the usual changes in attendees and teachers. We learned so much from each other thanks to the initial foundation provided by Reverend Funk.

Did the Bible Study bear fruit? The amazing result is that three members from that class went into the ministry. Two of them taught our class. All three went on to seminary as a second career. Each of them had a slightly different call to ministry, but it was inspirational to watch their spiritual growth and get reports on their seminary experiences. Jack Dutton was one of those teachers from 1995 to 2005. Looking back, you could see his growth and deepening understanding of the Bible.

I want to share how the Holy Spirit found pastors in a lumberyard, the food processing industry, on a ranch, a nursing home and finally the funeral industry. Often, others saw the spiritual gifts in those individuals and started encouraging and praying for them to consider the ministry.

Reverend Jack Dutton's Call Story

Since 1983, Jack had felt the call for ministry. His pastor saw the gifts and encouraged him. But as a young man with a growing family and a successful career in Arkansas, the idea of attending seminary didn't seem financially realistic. After moving to Topeka in the early 1990s, he became a Sunday school teacher at Countryside UMC in the class started by Reverend Funk. He felt teaching Sunday school was his gift, but gradually it wasn't enough. He was the operations manager for a lumberyard that had financial problems and had to close. He counseled and helped his employees find other jobs. This opened the door for Jack to enter the ministry. Countryside United Methodist Church senior pastor, Paul Mitchell offered him a staff position to develop spiritual growth ministries, which included a wide range of opportunities to serve others. It was understood that he would attend seminary.

Today, he is still pastoring and making a difference in the churches he serves. Jack and I would simply affirm that Rev. Edith Funk left a large spiritual footprint by starting one Bible study.

It makes me smile to remember that the twelve disciples were second-career pastors. Rev. Jack Dutton's call story illustrates the importance of finding creative ways to finance seminary. Pastor Paul Mitchell's approach allowed our church to help fund part of seminary and allowed Jack to serve his congregation in the process. Churches must be mindful to both spiritually and financially support those we encourage to attend seminary. Attending seminary would not be possible for many who experience the calling for ministry without charitable donations and scholarships.

I did a series of interviews with Rev. Warren Swartz for this book which were extremely insightful. Let me introduce Reverend Swartz, who is now in his late eighties. He had a distinguished career serving churches in Nebraska. He had the opportunity to build St. Marks UMC in Lincoln from a struggling church with seventy-eight members into a powerful church with more than 2,500 members. He served as a district superintendent in Nebraska supervising more than sixty churches for six years. In retirement, he served St. Paul UMC in Lincoln providing pastoral care and later did the same in Kansas as a pastor of congregational care in Topeka. His insights and perspective were instrumental in the preparation of this book. He recognized that the smaller churches are essential to nurturing young and second-career pastors.

Reverend Warren Swartz's Call Story

Rev. Warren Swartz grew up in Denver. His mother was a single parent. As a youth, he coincidentally attended the Warren United Methodist Church. This church provided a vital support system for their family and started his faith journey. The Warren UMC pastor, Dr. Lowell Swan, gave Warren encouragement and allowed him to be involved in youth activities. After Warren and Tag were married, they remained active in the church. Dr. Swan, along with others, recognized Warren's gifts for ministry. Dr. Swan also let Warren know that a generous member of the church had donated funds for those wishing to attend seminary. Generous funding made a career change possible for the Swartz family. Dr. Swan went on to be the president of Iliff School of Theology in Denver, where he also left a large spiritual footprint.

When Warren was called to ministry, he was working in sales for the Swift Company in Denver. Warren still insists Swift hams are the very best. That is a dedicated employee who hasn't worked for the company in more than sixty years! After prayer and encouragement, Warren went into see his boss to share his intentions of going to seminary and entering the ministry. Initially, his boss told him he was doing well and offered him a promotion to a larger route. Warren thanked him and announced he was starting seminary in the fall. To his surprise, his supervisor told him that he too was resigning to enter seminary in the fall. Amazing!

Obviously, not everyone has a Damascus Road experience like the apostle Paul or a burning bush like Moses, but the next two stories show the presence of the Holy Spirit in powerful ways.

Reverend Fritz Clark's Call Story

Countryside UMC had a pastor named Rev. Fritz Clark who was a successful rancher. He raised purebred Charolais cattle. He was president of the Kansas Charolais Association and served on several committees of the Kansas Livestock Association (KLA). This included serving as vice-chair of the Purebred Council of the KLA. He also led major committees in the American International Charolais Association. Close friends of his were what I would call "persistently invitational," regularly inviting Fritz and Jan to church. It was done in a positive way. Fritz was not regularly churched as a youth and described himself as an EC (Easter/Christmas attendee).

Fritz and his wife, Jan, began attending regularly with the positive influence of their friends and the nudge of the Holy Spirit. He served in several leadership positions in the church and was then asked to be on the Church Nominating Committee. Fritz accepted the position, assuming that he could avoid further committee work by appointing others. At the first meeting, he was "strongly pushed" to be the lay leader of the church, and the entire committee elected him into this vital leadership position, much to his chagrin.

The Holy Spirit showed up again when he was asked to coordinate a three-day revival at the Wamego United Methodist Church. Let's just say Fritz was not overly excited about helping coordinate and host the event, but he gladly met his responsibilities. On the last day, the evangelist presented a handout asking everyone to mark something they would change to assist them on their faith journey. It ranged from regular attendance in a Bible study, regular presence in church, improved giving, prayer chains, etc. The last option on the handout simply said, "I will consider ordained ministry." These words stood out to Fritz like they were written in boldface type or a neon sign, except they were the same size as the other options on the page. Fritz was shocked and uncomfortable. He quickly folded the sheet without marking it and put it in his pocket. For the next three years, Fritz tried to move past this invitation, but he had trouble sleeping at night as the Holy Spirit kept nudging him. He didn't talk to Jan about this struggle. He thought he had moved past this call until the Holy Spirit again gave him a shove in Virginia City, Nevada.

While on vacation, they were visiting a historic Catholic Church in Virginia City. As Fritz entered, he was "bathed in the Holy Spirit" and suddenly Fritz backed out of the church in awe. He knew he had been called to enter the ministry and could no longer ignore that invitation. It was an overpowering experience. Like Jonah and others in the Bible, Fritz had been resisting the call.

One immediate problem was how to exit the ranching business. He needed to sell three pieces of land and most of the cattle, but this was the height of the Rural Crisis in the 1980s. There was no demand for ranch land or cattle at the time. One day, an eighty-year-old rancher showed up in an old pickup and asked if the land was still for sale. Fritz said yes, and the gentleman paid cash for the land. Another parcel of land was purchased by a retiring auto dealer who had always wanted to own that piece of land. The only prospect for the last parcel was a school principal who wanted to farm but was hesitant to make such a major change in his life. Fritz's quiet brother, L. A. Clark, asked if he could make one last appeal to the principal. He was successful. It was sold. As for the cattle, Fritz received an unexpected call from a Texas rancher who liked his cattle and was ready to expand his herd. Four unlikely purchases, if not for the power of the Holy Spirit.

After seminary, Reverend Clark had a successful career in ministry. It wouldn't have happened without invitational friends, his family, his church, and the guiding hand of the Holy Spirit.

On July 17, 1981, the Hyatt Regency walkway collapse in Kansas City, Missouri, killed 114 and injured 216. Two walkways, one directly above the other, collapsed into the hotel lobby during a tea dance. It was one of the worst structural disasters in US history. Among the dead was Karla Woodward's mother. Overcoming her personal loss was one more step that led Karla to become an ordained deacon, serving others by teaching and providing powerful congregational care. In the UMC, a deacon has the authority to teach and proclaim God's Word, to lead in worship, assist in the administration of the sacraments of Holy Baptism and Holy Communion, and to perform weddings and funerals. Sometimes, they are called to serve as youth educators, congregational care leaders, missionaries, or in numerous other mission opportunities.

Rev. Karla Woodward's Call Story

Karla Woodward's mother was the loving caregiver for her family, helping take care of elderly aunts and her family. As a young five-year-old girl, Karla enjoyed visiting her aunt and talking to other residents in the nursing home. At age thirteen, Karla recalls a chaotic moment in a nursing home while her grandfather was dying. There were four patients sharing one room.

Karla's grandfather and family were crying and saying goodbye. Another resident was yelling while another resident with dementia, dressed in an open-air hospital gown, walked into the room and couldn't figure out how to lay down. He proceeded to stand up on his bed. Through the rays of sunlight of the venetian blinds, God called her to serve the fragile and elderly that day. She earned a BSN in nursing. When her mother died, the grief was overpowering, but the inspiration of her mother's legacy and the spirit of God comforted her. Karla knew that God was with her during this tragedy. She went on to get her master's degree in Social Gerontology.

Karla started attending the five-thirty Saturday evening service at the Church of the Resurrection in Leawood, Kansas. It is a church with a discerning culture of call lead by Reverend Adam Hamilton. Suddenly, Karla was surrounded by pastors and laity, encouraging her to attend seminary. Rev. Fran Manson and Rev. Lowell Thuma encouraged Karla to explore new ways to serve God. She was also nurtured by Rev. Karen Lampe and Rev. Yolanda Villa. While attending a Disciple Bible Study, her facilitator, Rev. Becky Johnson, told her she had the spiritual gifts to serve and should go to seminary. By being a discerning congregation, they gained an invaluable staff member. She served on staff at the Church of the Resurrection for ten years. Karla lead the Silver Link ministry for the frail as well as providing pastoral care as part of the pastoral care team. God is now using her gifts to provide amazing congregational care and make disciples for Jesus Christ.

During Lent, our church always uses a devotional study for each day. Some years, the members of the congregation write the devotionals with the scripture that fits. Several years ago, a recently retired UMC Pastor named Rev. Kent Melcher wrote this devotional sharing his call story to ministry. He graciously allowed me to share this inspirational story.

Reverend Kent Melcher's Call Story

After five years in Kansas, Julie and I had settled down to a pleasant family life in a comfortable home in Roeland Park. The house we bought there in 1976 still elicits wonderful memories. Sarah and Joshua were born while we lived there. We love our favorite photographs from that house: our kids in the backyard, the Christmas tree in the living room, and family and friends around our dinner table.

My "promising" job had turned into a comfortable living for us. We weren't rich by any means, but we had all the necessities of life. We kept the bills paid, and we could take time away to visit family and enjoy simple vacations with the kids.

In August 1980, I had just had the most profitable month of my sales career when I planned my monthly sales trip to southwest Missouri. Funeral directors in that part of the state bought from three small casket companies within a few miles. They could reorder, or special order, any product and receive it that day or the next. Our Kansas City warehouse could not compete with the quick service those companies provided, and our prices were higher (never mind that the quality of our product was also superior). I seldom got many orders from southwest Missouri.

That week surprised me. On Monday and Tuesday, customers gave me several orders. On Wednesday, I called on eight funeral directors. All eight ordered something: almost never did I have a day when every customer placed an order!

At the hotel that evening, as I filled out my daily sales report, I heard, almost audibly, these words: "When are you going to do what I want you to do?"

I had heard a call to ordained ministry several times in the past but had always resisted. "Surely you are mistaken, God. You can't possibly want me. I have too many flaws, too many sins, too many reasons why I can't do what you want me to do." But this time, for whatever reason, I could not resist the urging of the Holy Spirit.

I rearranged my Thursday and Friday schedules to call on my best customers on the way back to Roeland Park. I didn't tell my wife, Julie. I showed up in the driveway late Thursday afternoon. She said, "What are you doing home?" I said, "We have to talk."

Somehow, I knew it was the right thing to do, but it was still scary. I said at the time, it was like stepping off a cliff, and hoping someone would catch me. Two weeks later, I was enrolled at Saint Paul School of Theology. (How that all fell into place is a story that still amazes me!) At the first Saint Paul chapel service, I found myself sitting in a pew with tears of joy and hope running down my face.

Sometimes new beginnings happen because of the circumstances of life: a death in the family, the loss of a job, a job transfer to a new city, or health conditions that alter one's physical abilities. Such events can take us, unwillingly, by surprise, and when they do they can create anxiety and even fear.

Other times, as at that time in my life, a new beginning offers exciting new challenges that seem right, especially when we see them as opportunities for personal and spiritual growth.

Where is God calling you to a life of faithfulness and service to the reign of God? How will you respond?

This is another remarkable call story full of hope and joy serving the Lord. How are you personally answering the two questions posed by Rev. Kent Melcher?

Discernment Questions

After discussing the questions posed by Reverend Melcher, take time to reflect on your own church. Then continue to the following questions to further expand your outreach.

- How can you enrich the spiritual footprint of your church?
- Is your church willing to help fund a scholarship for a student who is considering the ministry or attending seminary?
- Would your church explore funding a summer internship for a youth interested in ministry?

Chapter 3

Great Unrealistic Expectations

How do we develop realistic expectations from the pews to experience a meaningful faith journey and partner with our pastors for successful ministry? I believe that the first thing is to realize that ministry is teamwork. God calls congregations to work together. Churches often struggle with unrealistic expectations. The congregation must understand that they are called to minister to each other, which includes the pastor. Some members of the congregation have expectations that the worship service is to entertain and impress them or that the pastor is the hired help. Ministry should be built on teamwork. It is a full contact sport if the church is serious about making disciples for Jesus Christ and making a difference in the lives of others. Was I positive, invitational, and affirming to others? This means coming to worship and small group study prepared to worship, with an open mind to learn and a joyful heart to share, prayerfully supporting your pastor and congregation. There are many ways to prepare for worship. Did you spend time praying or reading the scripture for that Sunday? Did you remember to invite a coworker, friend, or neighbor to church? Did you help deliver food or clothing to those in need? Did you to remember check on someone who had been ill that week, or offer someone a ride to church? Did you decide which mission effort you were going to volunteer for to serve others? There is no limit to the possibilities!

Are you holding expectations for your pastor that you or others could personally handle? Have you ever put yourself in the shoes of your pastor? Can you imagine standing behind the pulpit giving a sermon? Standing beside the bed of a dying person? Planning for and leading weekly Bible studies? Being available to the congregation twenty-four/seven? Relating to all generations of folks? Leading the youth group and teaching the little ones in VBS (Vacation Bible School)?

The fear of public speaking is one of the most common phobias. In college, I had two traumatic experiences behind a pulpit that provided me with a deep appreciation for all pastors. In the early 1970s, I was a student at Southwestern College in Winfield, Kansas. I was among the students recruited to go to forty United Methodist churches to thank them for supporting the college and share information about the benefits of attending a Christian college. I had experience in debate and forensics in high school, so I was comfortable with public speaking. I was assigned to speak at two churches. Fortunately, I only had five to seven minutes. During my insightful remarks, I apparently implied attending a Christian liberal arts college provided a superior education. (I am still not sure what I said to this day.) Afterward, I was pelted with well-deserved barbs implying they probably didn't know as much as me since they only attended small universities in Lawrence or Manhattan, Kansas. My personal favorite was, "I barely got through Harvard with my master's degree." Forty-five years ago, it didn't seem this funny. It was a learning experience and quickly eliminated any thoughts of going to seminary. It did remind me that standing and speaking is not an easy task, and we expect pastors to do it perfectly week after week.

Unfortunately, my second church presentation didn't go as well as the first. It was a small beautiful country church in Butler County just east of Wichita, Kansas. When I arrived, I was told I could have as much time as I wanted. That is never a good sign! That is especially true when you have only prepared for eight to twelve minutes, which included time for booing and/or standing ovations. There was one minor detail that I didn't learn until I arrived. It was the last Sunday for this church! It would be closing its doors forever after the service.

As a young college student, I wasn't ready for that fork, or rather dead end, in the road. As I started speaking, the first lady started sobbing, which continued throughout my inconsequential remarks. It gradually became a chorus. The longer I talked, the louder it became. (My wife, Donna, can confirm that the sound of my voice has also caused her to cry on numerous occasions.) At the end, I wasn't sure who was more traumatized: the twenty-five remaining members of the congregation or myself. I now realize that I had witnessed the death of a church. At the time, I felt like I helped kill a church, or at least didn't know how to revive it.

This experience provided me with a vivid illustration of the importance of pastoral leadership from the pulpit, the challenge of preaching along with the unexpected turns and twists that pastors face in presenting a weekly message. Can you imagine learning about a tragedy or disaster a few minutes before a worship service and praying to find the right words? As a young college student, I didn't have a prayer to help me affirm the service and ministry of that small church. Today I cringe when I hear unfair criticism of a pastor or a sermon and refrain from saying, "Can you do better?" I already know the answer for me.

My point is that pastors get immediate feedback, both good and bad, at least weekly. How is that for a way to finish your work week while serving as the hands and feet of Jesus Christ? Religion is so personal, and everyone has a slightly different understanding, which only increases the difficulty. Words will have a different meaning to an individual just starting their faith journey in contrast with someone who has studied the Bible for sixty years. This is also compounded by our diversity and life experiences.

How would you like to get graded every week in your job by individuals with many different viewpoints? In 2002, I attended the funeral for Dr. John Davis, who was my first optometrist when I moved to Topeka. He was a seventy-year member of his Baptist church. During the service, the pastor pointed out that Dr. Davis would always give him his bulletin marked up with comments on the music and the sermon immediately after the service. Obviously, some comments were good, and some pointed out differences of opinion. This can be a constructive way of nurturing pastors, but I prefer notes of encouragement. In interviewing pastors for this book, several mentioned that this was not unusual in the churches they served. Often, some bulletins with kind, nurturing, and inspiring remarks became cherished mementos of their ministry. At least three ministers mentioned that English teachers or professors often sent separate notes or letters afterward with numerous suggestions for improving their grammar and delivery.

Rev. Warren Swartz, as I mentioned in the second chapter, had a distinguished career serving churches in Nebraska. In one of his first sermons, Reverend Swartz shared that the local newspaper editor pointed out more than forty grammatical or documentation errors in the sermon. The key was that it wasn't done inappropriately but in an encouraging way that nurtured his professional growth. From that point on, Warren worked hard to use appropriate grammar and documentation of his sources in sermons. He viewed this as constructive criticism that nurtured and improved future sermons. The patience, insights, grace, and love from the smaller churches and communities where Warren served were essential for his future success in ministry. This was also a recurring theme in my interviews with other pastors and candidates for ordained ministry in the United Methodist Church. Sadly, there are a few churches that are not clergy friendly, where promising careers in ministry were unable to flourish and sometimes ended.

Congregations must always seek to be a clergy-friendly church that walks alongside the pastors with appropriate, nurturing comments and support. Rev. Rick Saylor shared that the first church he served in Pennsylvania "loved him into the ministry" for four years when he was starting his career. They demonstrated grace and patience while he was learning. Reverend Saylor's example is a perfect definition of a clergy-friendly church. Pastors of all ages, no matter how much experience they have behind the pulpit, need congregational care and prayerful support. Everyone needs encouragement and constructive feedback. Imagine the Madison Effect sending sixteen members into ministry and an ongoing culture seeking more to this day.

Each week, your pastor sees the faces of congregation members with a diverse number of needs and concerns. It may be the joy of the birth of a new child, the devastation of health issues, marital or family issues, job loss or a promotion, the overwhelming grief from losing a loved one, financial crisis, and various addictions or mental health challenges. These life-changing experiences are on the hearts of a congregation each week. Can you imagine having to prepare a weekly message to inspire and give hope to such a varied range of needs and emotions? Think about that for a weekly responsibility as you pray for your pastor, church volunteers, and church staff regularly.

Do you realize that too often it turns out that Sunday is the easiest day of the week if you are a pastor? The job description for a pastor is open-ended in many cases due to our "great unrealistic expectations." The challenges that our ministers face weekly go unnoticed or misunderstood. They range from hospital visits, premarital counseling, weddings, funerals, sermon preparation, Bible study, following up with visitors, and discussing end-of-life issues with families, to name a few.

Several years ago, a woman appeared in our church for the first time. After the eleven o'clock service, she told our senior pastor, Rev. Rick Saylor, that she needed to talk to someone about her cancer diagnosis. She didn't have a church family but looked to the church to provide passionate assistance and prayerful support in her despair. He prayed with her and gave her the assistance that she needed by being the hands and feet of Jesus Christ. Pastors have numerous interruptions of their schedules and unexpected opportunities to minister every week, and so does the congregation. *Laity and clergy alike need to always be ready to minister to strangers who enter their lives and churches in unexpected ways.*

Administrative Responsibilities

Another aspect to this discussion on pastoral responsibilities must include numerous administrative duties with church finances, staff supervision in larger churches, working with volunteers, committee meetings, and numerous other requests from the congregation which may or may not be reasonable. A difficult season of ministry are the sermons on the topic of financial giving and generosity. Congregations don't realize that most pastors regularly tithe and may often be among the top givers in their congregations. They are practicing what God calls all the faithful to do. We all need to work on improving our own financial generosity and challenge others to do the same.

How does your congregation celebrate the ministry of your pastor as God's faithful servant? For sure, don't forget to celebrate Clergy Appreciation Sunday. But that's only twenty-four hours of appreciation each year, whether our clergy need it or not! Congregations need to regularly send notes of encouragement to our pastors, volunteers, and staff, and always include them in our prayers. Great ideas could be to give gifts cards or a special gift, or how about a plate of cookies or fresh veggies from the garden? There is nothing that prohibits us from the care and support of clergy. Are you wanting to sign up for seminary by now?

Let's review this open-ended job description one more time. These duties also don't reflect regular meetings with district superintendents, clergy continuing education sessions, and conference meetings. Depending on the size of the church there are other routine responsibilities that I haven't yet mentioned, some of which might require training beyond seminary in counseling, psychology, business administration, or information technology. Some of these tasks might be the unlocking and locking up of the church, driving the van, getting someone to work on the air conditioning or heating system. Of course, this doesn't address the dreaded technology issues if the computers don't work or the sound system has problems or there are dead batteries in the microphones. My point is a simple one. *We want our pastors doing ministry, not tasks that can be accomplished by volunteers, ministry teams, and other ministry volunteers.*

Fortunately, God calls some among us with those backgrounds to volunteer or enter a second career in ministry just like the disciples. I seem to remember that Jesus called several fishermen, a tax collector, and a physician. On the Damascus Road, the apostle Paul—or, more accurately, Saul—was called to leave his work persecuting Christians. We don't always appreciate those providing ministry to us nor do we always recognize the unique gifts they offer us each week.

I must apologize for having painted this challenging picture of ministry to illustrate some of my concerns and frustration. In fairness, I must point out that all the clergy I interviewed said they have been blessed and found the ministry to be an amazing experience. Rev. Morgan Whittaker Smith summed it well: "For all its grumpy sides, being a pastor is an awesome privilege, and the majority of us love it most of the time. There are grouchy people in every career, but we get to do all kinds of amazing, sacred things others don't get to do or can even imagine. It's a worthwhile trade-off."

Clergy encounter amazing sacred moments referenced by Rev. Morgan Whittaker Smith during baptisms, hospital visits, and weddings. Pastor Charles Cryderman shared a moving story about a message on his answering machine when he arrived home late one evening. It was from the hospital and said that Bob was waiting to die until he sees you. As a young man, Bob had helped unload the bricks from the train on his horse-drawn wagon for his church. He unloaded them at the site where the church was being built. He repeated this process many times to finish. Without a doubt, he qualified as one of the cornerstones for his local church. When Rev. Cryderman arrived at the hospital, he told Bob that it was okay and prayed with him. Bob passed away quietly a few moments later, but he wanted assurance from his pastor.

Essential Nature of the Culture of the Call

United Methodist ministers agree to itinerate, which means they are under appointment by the Bishop of the Great Plains UMC annual conference and can be moved to other churches in Kansas and Nebraska as needed. They are our modern-day circuit riders sharing the Gospel. In some areas, they may serve several smaller churches. There are also clergy couples serving different churches a hundred miles apart, only seeing each other a few days a week. Others may be serving churches while their spouse has a job elsewhere. This can be a challenge for our pastors. Understanding itineracy strongly underscores the deep commitment of United Methodist clergy to serve churches. This is not always understood or appreciated by congregations. Congregations need to show support and flexibility for pastors in this situation.

This brings us to an essential culture-of-call question. Are we intentionally trying to discern and cultivate those within our congregations who have the gifts for ministry? The Madison Effect requires a concerted effort with prayer, encouragement, and watching for individuals blessed with the talents needed for ministry. Recognition of those being called is an essential step in the realization of the Madison Effect in any of our churches. This is followed by providing encouragement to explore what they might be called to do. Is it the pulpit or the mission field? Finally, it is vital that they be given leadership opportunities to grow, which means others need to be open and be willing to mentor them. Church leaders, pastors, mentors, and coaches need to discover ways to use the leadership gifts of those called, setting aside their own egos.

Becoming an Invitational Congregation

This is not an inclusive list, only my personal insights of things to avoid in the attempt to become an invitational church full of grace. I call it my personal pew pet peeves. Do you remember the welcoming grace-filled picture that Rev. Larry Fry painted of the Madison United Methodist Church as he was growing up? There were opportunities to serve others, everyone was welcome, and all enjoyed hospitality with each other. No church is perfect or without challenges. Yet I believe you would be less likely to hear some of these comments in a church like the Madison church.

1. "I haven't seen you for a while." A better way would be to say, "It is great to see you this morning," or ask how they have been. This will help to determine if they have been ill or having some other challenge. I really dislike the expression "I haven't seen you here before." This comment will

make a return visit to your church unlikely if they are a visitor and would offend someone who has been a member longer than you have been. Again, it is imperative that congregation members view themselves as ministers who should always be welcoming and practicing radical hospitality as discussed by Bishop Robert Schnase in his book *Five Practices of Fruitful Living*.

2. A second thing to think about is questioning the attendance of others or judging others based on having your own "nearly perfect" attendance record. Please stop it. It is imperative that all of us realize that everyone has commitments. This is especially true for young families who have activities for their children throughout the week. Weekends may be filled with gymnastics, music, dance, or sports, to name only a few of the multitude of the choices available. We should rejoice when families are able to attend church! I am so impressed when I see parents or grandparents bring a child to church even when they are dressed for a soccer game later in the day. How about those who work on weekends? On some Sundays at the 8:30 service, I see a pharmacist, named Cathy Fisher, leave a few minutes early before the closing hymn to make it to work on time. She has inspired our congregation for more than thirty years by leading mission trips and assuming other leadership roles. She helps arrange for food for the needy at Christmas and so much more. She is a powerful witness and inspiration to all of us. We are also inspired to see another faithful disciple who takes lunch hour from 11:00 to 12:00 on Sundays to attend church. My point is that I rejoice when I see members who work on the weekends but still make a special effort to worship.

3. One of the worst violations committed by loyal weekly members who see a friend visiting the church for the first time is when they say, "What are you doing here?" I am sadly an offender and I was so embarrassed. Before I could apologize, another longtime leader in our church came up

to the same individual and said the same thing. Always remember, United Methodists say, "Open hearts, open minds, and open doors." Let's actually practice it.

4. Have you ever heard someone say, "I can't hear over the baby crying," or "Those children won't stop talking," or "Why won't those children sit still?" I view the presence of infants and children as a sign of vitality of a church and an affirmation of God's creation. Why would we want to discourage young families with children from attending our services? Why would you ever say anything unkind or unwelcoming to young families? They are a part of the Christian family and they deserve our encouragement, support, and prayers. With church attendance declining, this behavior toward children is inappropriate. In fairness, I should point out that my fifteen-month-old grandson, Austin, has just started randomly screaming and then laughing. It is not cute after the second time, so we have utilized the family room during church on those occasions.

5. "We have always done it that way!" Cynically, I always wonder if that is good or bad! This comment is often heard when change occurs. Embracing and accepting change is hard for many of us. Remember, each pastor has their own style of worship, which is fine. In two years, you probably won't remember the differences, especially if you are my age! Unwillingness to embrace change means that your church may be missing opportunities for new ministry needed in today's world. It also means you are missing an opportunity for your own personal growth on your faith journey. Change can be good and is often needed to enhance ministry and our personal journey. Churches that won't change miss opportunities for new ministry and may not be around for the next generation. If your church is committed to seeking spiritual renewal and making new disciples of Jesus Christ, then your church will be seeking new opportunities and embracing change. When we interview candidates for ordination, I am always so impressed with some of the new

innovative approaches to various mission efforts created by partnering with their congregations. By taking action and creating new ministries, it energizes those congregations, because they have ownership of the ministry. It inspires those who have been passive disciples to leave the church building and go out and help others or encourage others who might be considering entering the ministry.

6. This next reflection involves rude and insensitive comments to pastors before or after services. Often, they are meant to be cute or funny. Let's start with inappropriate comments about their appearance. Why didn't you wear a robe for today's service even though it was 100 degrees outside and 110 inside the church? When I received a complaint about this issue while I served on our church personnel committee, my response was to ask if they wanted a dress code for the congregation! I would smile, and this ended the conversation with a smile back. My personal favorite is "Your shoes didn't match the color of your robe." Another comment is "Have you lost weight?" (implying the pastor needs to lose weight) or "Have you gained a few pounds?" Would you appreciate these comments in your workplace or while you were in church worshipping? Pastors are making a difference and ministering to us every week and they deserve better. If you spent Saturday finalizing your sermon while helping a family plan a funeral and visiting a member in a hospital emergency room Saturday night, how would you appreciate these insensitive comments that distract us from the real purpose of attending worship?

7. Then there are inappropriate expectations by complaining and asking the pastor about routine matters that laity can handle, like unlocking the church and janitorial duties. While I was greeting one Sunday, someone came to me saying a dog got sick outside the door and the church janitor needs to clean it up. I gladly cleaned it up, but we often miss the point, again, that we need to help around

the church wherever we see help is needed. Even if it is a messy job!

8. "Why are you sitting in my pew?" This is wrong on so many levels. The response should be saying good morning and being welcoming even if someone is sitting in your sacred pew. Get up, move around, and consider sitting in a new pew at least once every year. I don't want to be too radical, but what if you sat on the other side of the church? You might make some new friends or brighten the day of those you don't regularly sit among! Obviously, this is a silly joke, but it makes sense to meet as many members of the congregation as possible. I could see "New Pew Sunday" annually or monthly to remind us. Unfortunately, the first time I tried it, I was pelted by comments like "Are you lost?" or "Why are you punishing our side of the church?" Please try it, and at least half of the church will be happy. Recently, I attended the late morning service instead of my regular 8:30 service. It was a good opportunity to meet other members. I should mention that I did receive some ribbing. Comments included, "What did we do wrong?" The value of good-natured humor can't be underestimated in ministry or community worship.

9. The failure to recognize that your complaining, inaction, and unwillingness to help is part of the challenge, preventing meaningful ministry. No explanation is needed, but I will try anyway. This applies to nurturing new pastors to your church by giving them a fair chance and remembering to help rather than complain. Often, volunteers get so much more out of the experience than those they serve. It reinforces a sense of purpose in your life when you volunteer, often resulting in life-changing experiences. It brings the scriptures to life. Sometimes I feel guilty teaching a Bible study because I get so much more out of it during my preparation. Giving others the opportunity to lead or share in teaching is essential to assure the vitality of our churches. I am always looking to give others the opportu-

nity to lead. We will explore volunteering in more depth in another chapter.

10. The unwillingness to compromise, learn, or even discuss new opportunities is something we need to consider. This results in splits in churches. My Southern Baptist friends humorously call this church growth when one faction leaves to start their own church over a theological debate or dispute. We see theological debates throughout the Old and New Testament and for more than two thousand years since. Does the method of baptism make a profession of faith less worthy? Theological debates are inevitable over every subject, especially communion. Thomas Welch gave us grape juice to solve the concerns within the Methodist church over serving wine to address alcoholism. As a layperson, my goal is make disciples for Jesus Christ and not judge anyone. Jesus ministered to the poor and those forgotten or ignored by society. My worst fear is becoming a Pharisee or Sadducee! In smaller churches, or patriarch/ matriarch churches, it can be a challenge when some of the founding influential families may withhold financial resources to block new ministry initiatives. It is important that everyone is open to the needs of the congregation, the community, and new opportunities. All of us must be educated on the benefits and challenges of any new ministry. Obviously, this can be a problem in churches of any size. If changing the order of worship or using a screen is too much of a technological change for you, then new approaches to ministry or worship can face resistance and discourage clergy from offering needed change and exploring new opportunities. It involves putting aside egos. This is true for laity and pastors. Let's not discourage dynamic new pastors who could leave the ministry before their skills are fully realized. The laity and clergy must not put their personal needs and biases first. This includes comparing pastors to each other. I dislike hearing "Pastor John was my favorite." I realize

it is human nature, but one must embrace the gifts of each pastor. Fortunately, I consistently see churches with new growth and exciting ministries who supported new pastors in their fruitfulness projects for ordination (clothing banks, food pantries, and other ministries addressing unmet needs). Churches of any size willing to explore new ministries and change are showing growth and renewed vigor through Bible study and involvement in new missional endeavors. If your church has limited resources, then focus on only one or two ministries, and do them well to build momentum.

11. I couldn't limit myself to ten, like Moses (actually God) and David Letterman. Please stop the unrealistic expectation of telling our pastors we need more members, more young families, a new roof, building expansion, and an increase in the number of mission trips. This is the responsibility of the congregation as they live out their mission statement. Don't tell the pastor to go do it, because it is our responsibility together as a congregation. Laity are the vital link to make ministry happen. Other churches say, "Let's hire someone to do it for us." It doesn't work without volunteers. Dr. Art Queen taught me this statement about volunteering: "Everybody can't do everything, but everybody can volunteer to do something." It is so true. Volunteering can indeed be an opportunity to find joy!

The other aspect is that the days of expecting others to walk into your front door are limited so becoming an invitational congregation is essential. Leaving the church to serve your neighborhoods, community, and the world is essential. Growing congregations go to where the people are, to serve their needs and minister to them. The Neighboring Movement and Fresh Expressions affirm the need to reach beyond the walls of our churches. They connect individuals and neighbors together while revitalizing churches and communities.

It is vital that each church develop and nurture a culture that encourages pastors along with laity to look forward to serving your church. Our goal is to be viewed as a clergy-friendly church. This means avoiding these roadblocks to becoming a more invitational and encouraging place where everyone serves in some capacity.

Discernment Questions

To avoid unrealistic expectations, church leaders need to be continually asking these discernment questions:

- Are you coming with a joyful spirit to truly experience a community of faith, to pray about the challenges and the blessings in your life? If so, how do you help others to experience this joy?
- How do you listen with an open heart and accept challenges from the pulpit and other places?
- How does your church welcome new visitors each week?
- What changes need to be made to this process to be even more invitational? Are you assuming there will be visitors each week?
- What steps will you take to train the congregation to regularly invite and bring friends, family, and neighbors to your services?
- In what ways are we holding ourselves accountable and volunteering to assure effective ministry is occurring in our churches instead of suggesting that the pastor or someone else do it?
- Are you applying realistic expectations to your pastor that you could personally handle in your own work setting or personal situation?
- We want our pastors doing ministry, not tasks that can be accomplished by volunteers, ministry teams, and pewsters. Has your congregation taken steps to avoid this pitfall?

Chapter 4

Effective Ministry Partnerships

One of my favorite stories about how easy it is for congregations to become distracted comes from former Great Plains United Methodist Church Bishop Rev. Scott Jones. He reminded us to focus on the "main thing," which is making disciples for Jesus Christ. He recalled a story about a long, tedious argument in one of the first churches he served. It was over where to plug in the coffeepot after some new construction. Finally, he blurted out, "God doesn't care where you plug in the coffeepot." The point is that churches inadvertently lose focus over hundreds of minor petty issues. In this chapter, I will examine some strategies to stay focused on the mission to which God calls your congregation.

Creating effective ministry partnerships requires excellent communication between clergy and the congregation. During my forty years of attendance at Countryside United Methodist Church, every pastor and associate pastor reinforced that all are on a faith journey. Each pastor provided essential pieces and steps for my journey as a Christian. I cherish what each pastor taught me, how they encouraged my growth, and how they challenged me to be a follower of Jesus Christ. They shared their special gifts for ministry beyond preaching from the pulpit. For some, it was teaching Bible study. For others, it was pastoral care, counseling, or church administration.

In the Great Plains United Methodist Church, the bishop and his cabinet, composed of district superintendents (who may supervise local churches), appoint and move pastors to the various churches in Kansas and Nebraska. In an appointive system, it may seem like a shotgun wedding as the cabinet tries to match pastors to the needs of various churches. In reality, it is a time for renewal for the incoming pastor and for the new church he or she will serve. Neither can succeed without working and partnering with the other. It starts with effective partnerships between the pastor and the Staff Parish Relations Committee (SPRC) in each church.

The SPRC is responsible for personnel issues and assuring communication between the pastor and the congregation. *The Book of Discipline* also provides this direction by sharing that "in conducting its work, the committee shall identify and clarify its values for ministry. It shall engage in biblical and theological reflections on the mission of the church, the primary task, and ministries of the local church."

What are your church's values for ministry? It is probably in your mission statement, providing your church has one. District superintendents have told me that 20–25 percent of the sixty-plus churches they supervised don't have a mission statement. Even when they encouraged churches to develop a mission statement, it was ignored. A mission statement answers the question about what God is calling your congregation to do. Why does your congregation exist? Without an understanding of where God calls the church, it is impossible to go there. Scripture provides clarity and direction. There are many passages that clarify values and direction for ministry. One of my favorites for staff parish committees comes from Colossians 3:12–13: "You must clothe yourselves with compassion, kindness, humility, gentleness, and patience. Be tolerant with one another whenever any of you has a complaint against someone else. You must forgive one another just as the Lord has forgiven you." This doesn't mean that you don't have to make hard personnel decisions nor have difficult discussions, but it does provide a compassionate framework for these conversations. There are so many powerful passages in the Bible that lend themselves to defining your church's values for ministry. The challenge is to focus on one or two. The next time you attend a church wedding, funeral, or special event in another church, please take a moment to look at their bulletin board and materials. You will see beautiful mission statements lifting different Bible passages and inspirational ministries. You just may come away inspired and renewed.

While it might sound like fun to review all seventeen duties in the United Methodist Church *Book of Discipline*, let's turn our focus at this time to some strategies to fulfill these duties successfully! After serving on the Countryside UMC Staff Parish Relations Committee, serving as chair of the personnel committee and serving on the Great Plains Board of Ordained Ministry, I have identified ten keys to successful ministry partnerships. These keys require that the congregation always remember they are ministers to each other and are willing to leave the walls of the church to serve. We must remain focused on our mission to make disciples of Jesus Christ for the transformation of the world. *The Book of Discipline* defines the mission as follows: "The mission of the Church is to make disciples of Jesus Christ for the transformation of the world. Local churches and extension ministries of the Church provide the most significant arenas through which disciple-making occurs."

The first key is a well trained Staff Parish Relations Committee. In the United Methodist Church, the Staff Parish Relations Committee (SPRC) is responsible for communication between the pastor and the congregation. The Staff Parish Relations Committee is where staff and congregational interests are integrated to focus on the mission of the church. The SPRC serves the "church governing board" in an advisory capacity related to personnel administration. It does not exist to provide managerial or leadership oversight to the staff team. That is the responsibility of the senior pastor. It starts with effective Staff Parish Relations Committees, who supervise the pastor(s). I found service on the SPRC to be a joy and a blessing. However, sometimes they must deal with conflicts beyond simply setting the salary and the annual evaluation of the pastor. This means members have been through an orientation that carefully outlines their responsibilities, remembering that confidentiality is required to be effective.

There should be guidelines and a procedure on how SPRC members handle concerns or questions from the congregation. When there are inquiries, it is important to let folks know you are listening and that you will share their concerns with the SPRC. There needs to be an appropriate and timely response. It is critical that SPRC members are on the same page in terms of handling inquiries. They need to work cooperatively with the pastor to address concerns. Communication should be done in a nurturing way to assure an appropriate response that doesn't create more misunderstandings but instead dispels them.

The second key is assessing each other's strengths and weaknesses. It starts by having an honest assessment by the congregation and the new pastor of the strengths and areas of challenges. This helps the pastor realize where the congregation needs assistance, thus enabling an effective partnership. What does your church do well, and what ministries are flourishing? Where does the church need to improve? The same questions should be asked of the pastor, so the Staff Parish Committee knows where the pastor may need assistance. These are not easy conversations, but they are so fruitful. It is vital to ask if you can be of assistance to create vital ministry. Be specific! Pastors may need assistance from time to time, and the Staff Parish Committee needs to find potential resources. A plan must be developed to annually address the identified strengths and areas for growth. Monitoring progress is essential to the church in fulfilling their mission statement. The key is a cooperative partnership with the pastor and the congregation, which creates and sustains effective ongoing ministry.

In this process, please don't forget to include an associate pastor, if you have one. It is critical that they have a defined role and job description that the congregation clearly understands. In visiting with pastors from all types of churches, I have met many who were frustrated serving as an associate pastor because their responsibilities were unclear, and they had little supervisory oversight. SPRCs should be sure that proper collaboration and oversight occurs between senior pastors and associate pastors. I pray the days are over when the senior pastor simply delegates tasks or responsibilities they dislike to the associate pastor. The gifts of associate pastors need to be utilized and cultivated to achieve more opportunities for ministry and enhance existing ones. Associate pastors will become senior pastors sooner if their gifts for ministry are utilized and refined through mentoring.

The third key is for churches with staff members to have and follow a personnel policy. The policy should be reviewed and updated regularly. Church employees need to be given a copy along with their job description when hired. They should be asked to sign a paper acknowledging it has been given to them. The signature indicates willingness to follow it. The SPRC needs to read the policies and refer to the document when making personnel decisions. I know it sounds outrageous, but following your own policies actually works.

The fourth key is professional development opportunities for your pastors. The Great Plains Conference of the United Methodist Church expects pastors to have essential continuing education (CE) to maintain competency and encourage lifelong learning. SPRCs are asked to budget for annual CE for their pastors. This prepares your pastor to not only serve your congregation but also for future ministerial appointments. Church-funded continuing education helps pastors learn the latest information and improve their skills for ministry. Often, the missing accountability piece is that the pastor should update SPRC and report on what was learned at CE events and how it will be applied or implemented into the church ministry.

What about professional development opportunities for more extensive renewal or training events where the pastor may be gone for a week or more? Is your Staff Parish Relations Committee willing to fund a substitute pastor to preach for an additional week or two in your budget? Some staff parish committees say they won't invest in this training event because the pastor might not be serving their church in a few years. This is a short-sighted view in an appointive system. Even if pastors are appointed to another church, those skills may help them inspire someone to enter ministry and become your pastor in ten or twenty years. Countryside has been blessed with three of our own members serving as associate ministers as they entered ministry and attended seminary. Never doubt the Madison Effect or how the Holy Spirit works.

The fifth key is assuring that the pastor is taking time for self-care to avoid burnout. How is this accomplished? First, it is imperative that your pastor takes vacation time. Second, the church must make a conscious attempt to honor time off for your pastor on the days they select for rest and renewal as much as humanly possible. Deaths and hospital visits make this difficult, but allowing time away is important. Third, it ties back to key four, allowing renewal time for continued learning. This provides renewal and a battery recharge with new insights and perspective. Finally, pastors need to be in an accountability group of their peers to discuss ministry and the challenges they may encounter. This is a necessary aspect of assuring self-care and realizing other pastors face the same opportunities and challenges. Staff Parish Relations Committees must intervene if congregation members are making unrealistic requests of their pastors. Pastors need to able to say no. Last time I checked, there are still only twenty-four hours in a day. Clergy shouldn't hesitate to notify their SPRC if these concerns arise. We need to allow flexibility in the pastor's schedule, so spouses and families have some time together.

The sixth key is to appropriately welcome new clergy and their families into your church family. There should be no limits to your creativity and Christian love in this process. We had a district superintendent who encouraged churches to provide a fully stocked refrigerator for the next minister's family. Several churches sent surveys to incoming pastors asking if they had food allergies, favorite foods, etc. Some were very extensive with types of milk, preferences for bread, or brands of coffee. When the new pastor's family arrived, they had a fully stocked refrigerator and kitchen. Please do not overwhelm the pastor while moving into the church office and getting settled. Staff parish should organize "get acquainted" sessions and opportunities to meet the new pastor in homes of pewsters in various neighborhoods and special events at the church.

The seventh key is that Staff Parish Relations Committees need to be a non-anxious presence in your church. This means to be a good listener and not overreact to complaints. Rev. Fritz Clark always reminded us to be a non-anxious presence. Remember the passage from Colossians that references compassion and tolerance in addressing concerns. Identifying the difference between minor concerns and serious concerns is not always easy. Some examples might explain what Rev. Clark is saying about being a positive presence.

There may be concerns that the minister didn't come visit them in the hospital. I always ask how they are feeling and doing since their hospitalization. Then I ask them if they had let the church know they were hospitalized. Did someone from the church ministry team come see them? Never overreact to minor complaints but always listen carefully and politely. Many times, someone listening is all that is needed or wanted. Be sure to update the pastor about any concerns or issues that may arise.

This issue shouldn't be limited only to the Staff Parish Relations Committee members. Being a non-anxious presence applies broadly to other church leaders, adult education teachers, and pewsters. What can pewsters do to be a non-anxious presence? First, don't get involved in gossip or petty disputes unless it is to be a calming influence. Simply ask if they have visited with the pastor about a concern or question. Second, accepting invitations to look at new opportunities for mission and be a member of a small group studying the Bible can help. This allows you to redirect any negative energy toward the mission of the church. Third, always ask yourself: are we making disciples for Jesus Christ and living out our church's mission statement? I also ask them to pray and give thanks to those leaders.

The eighth key is to always remember that we are called to make disciples for Jesus Christ and not be distracted by our differences. At the beginning of this chapter, I pointed out that Bishop Scott Jones reminded us to keep our focus. Remember the story about his first church where there was a dispute about where to plug in the coffeepot after construction. He finally told them God didn't care where the coffeepot was plugged in. This story is instructive for SPRC members when addressing questions and concerns from the congregation. Our fruitfulness needs to be measured in baptisms; youth confirmation classes; increased numbers attending Bible study, mission work, and vacation Bible school; and effective small groups.

Several years ago, Countryside UMC hosted a summer intern who shadowed our pastors when he was exploring going into ministry. The summer internship confirmed this young man's call to ministry. We had a church family graciously provide housing. Would your church consider offering a summer intern a three-month funded position for a potential seminary student? How about collaborating with other churches to fund an intern? Does your church already provide a summer intern to help with your youth program? A well supervised youth program intern can prove to be an invaluable investment for any church in reaching young people. It is an opportunity for the intern to develop their leadership skills for the future either as a pastor or as a church leader. Recall that Rev. Larry Fry was given this opportunity on his road to ministry.

The ninth key is showing kindness and appreciation. There should be an ongoing employee appreciation and recognition program beyond annual pay raises or bonuses. Do you provide gift certificates for special occasions or Clergy Appreciation Sunday? Do you include the entire staff in some of these appreciation endeavors? Some SPRCs provide food and snacks for staff during Christmas and Easter Services. This is especially needed if they have multiple services. There should be no limit to your creativity in providing concert tickets, bookstore gift certificates, or restaurant gift cards for pastors and staff birthdays. You might consider giving tickets to sacred spaces like seeing the Kansas City Chiefs in Arrowhead Stadium, Kansas City Royals in Kaufman Stadium, or places that are special in your community. Or what about tickets to a concert or movie? Sometimes nonmonetary gifts may be as thoughtful. Arrange acts of kindness by babysitting, running errands, and other expressions of support. Handwritten notes or electronic communications with thank-you notes and letters of encouragement can be used to nurture your staff.

Recently, we had a new pastor come to lead us, but his wife had to stay in Wichita for a year to finish her teaching obligation. A member of the congregation organized other members and groups within the church to send her care packages and notes of encouragement each month.

In smaller churches with no paid staff, it is important that your volunteers are regularly acknowledged, because they are essential for those churches. Some churches regularly encourage members to give testimonials thanking volunteers who cared for them or served them. Others do it throughout the year during church services and some share thank-you notes in newsletters or church bulletins. Volunteers must be recognized and cared for by their congregations as we are ministering to each other. They are an invaluable resource which we must never take for granted. I can't find any prohibitions in the Bible preventing applause after a musical selection nor kind words to volunteers before, during, or after church services. I also believe there is no prohibition on feeding choirs, organists, and musicians. I'm not sure about whispering thanks during the sermon! Kind words and notes of appreciation are never inappropriate, along with a sweet treat or gift card.

The tenth key is that the congregation should regularly laugh and pray for each other, the pastor, and staff. I always remember the old joke that if churches were perfect you wouldn't be a member. Humor is an important aspect of all ten keys to successful ministry partnerships. If we can laugh and even cry with each other, it helps assure success. We must remember to pray for each other, the pastor, and staff regularly in small groups and Bible studies. I have learned so much from other pewsters about how to pray in small groups. I now say a silent prayer for the emergency response personnel, law enforcement officers, ER staff, and those being helped when I hear sirens.

Cathy Wrenick was leading a Sunday morning class and shared that she found time to pray sitting at stop lights. I have found her comment to be so powerful and an amazing way to relieve stress. I can tell you it works better if you keep your eyes open while praying and driving! Recently, I nearly had a relapse. I almost honked at the car ahead of me after waiting more than ten seconds to move after the light turned green. Donna stopped me before I honked at the timid student driver in front of me! It works while standing in lines at a store. When I have delays, I now use the time to pray silently and thank God for the opportunity to have time to pray. If you are waiting in a doctor's office, this allows time for prayer, Bible study, and reading to prepare for a Sunday school class. We can learn so much from one another if we listen.

Finally, I would encourage the use of a checklist for SPRCs around the ten keys outlined in this chapter. If you don't like mine, please develop your own and share it with others. It is critical that you use it throughout the year as a reference.

Chapter 5

Here I Am, Send Me (Isaiah 6:8)

We have explored the first two aspects of the Madison Effect. The first was the realization by parishioners of the need to create a culture of call to ministry by identifying those with the gifts to be a pastor through congregational discernment. The second was remembering to nourish and to care for those called to pastoral ministry in our churches.

The third aspect of the Madison Effect is through engagement of the ministry volunteers and pewsters. We are going to explore our understanding of laity engagement. It starts with examining how it looks when congregations work together to serve those around them through a culture of volunteering. Stated simply, this is the congregation living out a culture of call that provides meaningful discernment and recognition of gifts in those who have indications of being called by God into pastoral ministry. The Madison Effect can inspire us!

God uses ordinary and imperfect folks to do amazing ministry. We often resist the call or ignore opportunities that come our way, whether it is to become a pastor or a lay volunteer. I am always overwhelmed by the imagery of God using a stuttering shepherd who had murdered an Egyptian overseer to lead his people out of bondage. Moses kept resisting as God spoke to him from the burning bush telling him to confront Pharaoh and lead the Exodus. While we may never encounter God speaking to us through a burning bush, each of us may receive divine inspiration or a subtle nudge from the Holy Spirit that reveals an opportunity to check on someone, send a card of encouragement, or volunteer for a mission project.

Kansas weather is notorious for drastic temperature changes. On one "typical" Kansas day the morning temperatures were in the 60s and by late afternoon drastically dropped into the 30s and sleeting. My daughter, Allyson, was driving by a bus stop and noticed a young mother holding her infant. Neither had coats or protection from the storm. Allyson turned around and went back. She gave the young lady her umbrella, a blanket, and took off her young son's coat for the child. Our grandson, Jaxon, cried all the way home in his car seat, not completely understanding what had happened. When I asked why she stopped, Allyson said it was her turn to help a stranger. It was just the right thing for her to do in that moment. An example of being nudged by God to use our gifts and resources for others.

Another example of a spiritual nudge comes from my wife, Donna. She had taught in the Shawnee Heights School District for many years and had a selected route to her school. For some reason she found herself driving a different route to her school on a road that was out of the way. She came upon a serious car accident. Quickly she pulled over. All the time she was slowing down and pulling over she was arguing with an inner dialogue that she should not stop as she had no medical training or first aid supplies, and a patrol car was already present on the scene. Then she found herself getting out of her car and getting into the wrecked car! All this time the inner debate between "Why are you doing this?" versus "Do this" continued. Immediately, as she sat inside the car with the trapped driver, she realized it was a coworker from her school. Donna held her hand and prayerfully comforted her until the paramedics could finally free her from the wreckage. She had numerous broken bones, including her pelvic bone, and was in tremendous pain. Afterward, Donna drove to school and told the staff about the accident. It was then that Donna broke down, trembling in shock. It was if she had been sheltered from the trauma while she was needed to comfort her friend. She realized that the Holy Spirit had redirected and guided her to help a friend in crisis. The Madison Effect in action!

Answering those nudges requires awareness followed by engagement. It is essential to create and maintain a culture of call to volunteer and serve others. All churches need to be exploring how to mentor, recruit, and train ministry volunteers to be future congregation leaders. One key is offering ministries that make a difference and giving opportunities for others to serve in those ministries. There are literally thousands of ministries that have moved passive pew sitters into active ministry. There are many ministries that can focus on providing food and clothing for their communities and others around the world. These ministries were created by ordinary laypeople and their churches to address local needs. This creates the essential components of responding to God through ownership and enthusiasm for those ministries.

John Wesley says it best: "Catch on fire with enthusiasm and people will come for miles to watch you burn." Volunteers are needed to stoke the fires for vibrant ministry. There is nothing more beautiful than a church afire with the enthusiasm for meaningful ministry! Dedicated volunteers are essential and one of our most precious resources for fruitful ministry.

It starts with congregations trying to live out and renew their congregational vows. We are reminded of these vows after a baptism or when we welcome new members into the United Methodist Church. Reflect on these vows in the broader context and culture of laity engagement and volunteering. The congregational vow states: "We give thanks for all that God has already given you and we welcome you in Christian love. As members together with you in the body of Christ and in this congregation of the United Methodist Church, we renew our covenant faithfully to participate in the ministries of the Church by our prayers, our presence, our gifts, our service, and our witness that in everything God may be glorified through Jesus Christ."

These words are easy to say, but the vow is difficult to live out. God calls each of us to faithfully share our prayers, our presence, our gifts, our service, and our witness in a meaningful way. Prayer is essential if we are going to minister to each other. We must pray for each other, check on each other and care for one another. This responsibility becomes real each week when we see the "concerns list" of those seeking our prayers, which gives us perspective on the importance of prayer and what really matters. Praying for your pastor, staff, church volunteers, and those on the concerns list is essential. Worshiping as a church family allows congregational prayers for others while improving our understanding of scripture, challenging us to move out into God's world to serve and share the good news of Jesus Christ and transform the world!

In the pre-cell phone era of the late 1970s, I vividly remember a short prayer about whether to minister to someone I encountered on the side of the road. It was very late when I was driving back to Topeka on the Kansas turnpike. There had been a series of incidents involving drivers who picked up hitchhikers and then were assaulted and robbed. One victim nearly died. Law enforcement had issued warnings not to pick up hitchhikers under any circumstances. While trying to stay awake, I suddenly encountered the image of a man in the dark with his thumb out, gripping what looked like a Bible. I whizzed on by. It was a cold November night with the temperatures dropping into the low 30s. I couldn't remember if I had seen an abandoned car. There might have been one back several miles, but I wasn't sure. I slowed down and asked God what to do. I prayed that it would be the right thing to help and sought God's protection. I literally decided to place my faith in what I thought was another man's Bible, which I wasn't even sure I saw. What would the Good Samaritan do? I stopped and slowly backed up. I was trying to determine if he was alone before I unlocked the door. The latest assaults had involved several individuals working together to rob motorists. I unlocked the door and let him into my car. We were two strangers scared to death of each other in total darkness on a deserted highway. Each praying for their own safety. Imagine my relief when he shared that he was a minister whose car had broken down. We had a pleasant conversation while I took him to his Topeka home. God answered both of our prayers. Too often we wait to pray until we have a serious personal challenge like the loss of a loved one or health problem. We need to be praying regularly for others and thanking God for the many blessings that God has given us rather than taking them for granted. God and the Madison Effect inspires me to constantly work on improving my daily prayer time, which is inconsistent at best.

The presence promised in our vows includes regular participation in worship in our community of faith. Worship reminds us of the importance of ministering to others. It challenges us to grow in our faith. Worship should be a joyful experience that we look forward to each week. It is my reset button and a respite from the hectic world. Before and after worship, I see individuals comforting someone who has lost a loved one and others celebrating with those who have a new child or grandchild. Worship often includes joy, music, laughing, and sharing a tearful moment. There should always be plenty of room for positive and affirming laughter. Humor is often needed to deal with the challenges in our lives. Humor allows us to have joy yet stay grounded in the faith. Our presence is the foundation of congregational discernment. Faithfully participating allows us to experience God's presence and meet and know each other in meaningful ways that might lead someone into the ministry.

The vow of sharing our gifts seems straightforward. Yet I see several types of gifts beyond generously giving of our financial resources through an annual pledge or tithe to the church. Financial commitments are necessary so that consistent ongoing ministries and clergy leadership can be maintained. The fact that our pastors donate to our churches and may be one of the church's larger donors should inspire the rest of us to give. Remember that we are blessed to be a blessing to others. When congregation members demonstrate financial stewardship and generosity, it helps churches develop a realistic budget for ministry. I realize that not everyone may be able to be as generous as they might wish due to numerous circumstances. Always remember gifts also include your invaluable time and talents.

How did the Madison church do this? Pastor Larry Fry described the many social events and fundraisers which created opportunities for generous hospitality and enjoyment in each other's company. Is the discernment process more difficult today with so many other commitments and opportunities available for us? How did they support training for those who were called from their congregation into ministry? In recent years, they offered a young man, whom they believed had the gifts for ministry, some financial assistance to attend college. It is a challenge to all churches to give some financial assistance and scholarships to congregation members seeking further education.

I have attended several seminars on giving led by J. Clif Christopher, a United Methodist pastor. He is a nationally recognized expert on financial stewardship and giving for church budgets and capital campaigns. Reverend Christopher shows congregations how to avoid pitfalls around financial stewardship and giving. His first book is entitled *Not Your Parents' Collection Plate*. I would recommend it to church leaders, generosity teams, and finance committee members. I look forward to reading his newsletter and updates each month. If you are interested in his free newsletter, you can go to the Horizons Stewardship website at https://horizons.net/giving365/ to subscribe.

Now let's focus on the concept of service and witness. Our congregational vow states "our service, and our witness that in everything God may be glorified through Jesus Christ." Both require a culture of volunteering to serve and witness to others. I see "our service" and "our witness" as almost interchangeable. When we respond, is it through our service, our witness, or both? It certainly requires congregational discernment and an invitational willingness to involve others. All churches need to be prayerful in exploring how to mentor, recruit, and train ministry volunteers to be future congregation leaders. This process often starts in small groups, Bible studies, or ministry teams. One key is offering ministries that make a difference and provide opportunities for others to learn more of God's call and serve in those ministries.

Let's examine what a culture of call to volunteer looks like through the eyes of a ministry volunteer. One of the inspirational interviews for this book was with Rev. Warren Swartz and his wife, Tag. We discussed Warren's call to ministry in the second chapter. They are in their late eighties now and remain full of energy and Christian love. They both fit my definition of successful disciples and illustrate that there is no age discrimination in ministry! Both symbolize how all disciples should seek to be active church volunteers, helping others grow in their faith and in service to their church. They attend and help teach adult education classes, they also volunteer to help various ministries. Recently the Swartz home was opened to thirty members of our United Methodist Youth. During Vacation Bible School, they were both actors in costume sharing Bible stories with the children. They were inspiring to watch, and their enthusiasm was contagious. If Warren didn't say a line with enough energy or skipped a phrase, she would correct him in a loving way. Warren's response was, "I am eighty-eight years old. What do you expect?" The children loved them. When you ask Tag to do something, she does it, and often more than what was asked. She even volunteers in the church office one day a week. After their children were grown, she became a nurse and provided compassionate care to her patients. Today, Tag still helps with blood pressure clinics at our church. It is a joy to speak with them, and I always come away inspired. Another example of how the Madison Effect becomes real!

In 1896, Rev. Charles Sheldon published a book entitled *In His Steps*, which has now sold 30 million copies. The book is about a minister who challenged his congregation to ask this question before doing anything: "What Would Jesus Do?" (WWJD). In 1900, Rev. Charles Sheldon was given the opportunity to publish the *Topeka Daily Capital* newspaper for one week as Jesus would have done it. If Tag Swartz is asked to provide a cake for a fundraiser, she will cheerfully ask if you needed two cakes. When my wife, Donna, and I now discuss how we can help with a ministry, we now ask WWTD, "What would Tag do?" Every church has these amazing saints who model Christian character for us by demonstrating their service and witness. Church leaders modeling both service and witness is essential. I can't think of a better way to illustrate our congregational vow of "our service and witness" than mentoring others. That is what the Madison Effect reveals to us.

We can see excellent examples of "sharing our service and witness" from those who use their talents or hobbies for meaningful ministry. I think about members who share their skills of woodworking and carpentry to help around the church, building ramps for homes of those in wheelchairs or with disabilities. I see God's gardeners working around our church, or the youth starting a community garden. I see amazing sewing and artwork used for inspiring worship banners. Even those who may be homebound or living in a nursing home inspire us by calling to check on others or sending cards for those with health challenges or concerns. There are teams going to help serve food at the mission and so much more. There are openings for volunteers to drive congregation members to church or doctors' appointments. Helping someone once or twice a month makes a difference. Simply put, laity engagement means seeing a need and addressing it.

Those who generously share their musical talents are a constant source of inspiration at Countryside UMC. I see churches of all sizes using everything from praise bands to those using recorded music to inspire. The voices of our children and youth accompanied by their instrumental skills provide some of the most inspiring music to me. These children and youth are learning how to be faithful disciples by sharing the gift of music. I have often wondered how much money could be raised if I promised to never play the piano for a worship service. Incidentally, I don't play the piano or even remember "Chopsticks." My last piano lesson was at age eight, and the teacher decided to stop giving lessons after I quit! My point is to be thankful for those who share their gifts and remember to say thanks. I would never violate John Wesley's directive to "sing lustily and with good courage." This applies no matter your level of talent!

A powerful illustration of using a hobby or talent was a prayer shawl ministry started by Kerry Storey and other ladies at Countryside UMC. I didn't realize that we had the ministry until shortly before my wife, Donna, became ill. We had numerous tests run and were sent to the Mayo Clinic in Rochester, Minnesota. Eventually, Donna had surgery and was hospitalized for more than a month. The prayer shawl ministry team gave her one of the shawls after they prayed for Donna. Donna had some difficult weeks, but when she wrapped that shawl around her it was so comforting. It was like she was getting a hug from God and being surrounded by the Countryside congregation. It was so powerful. Obviously, the visits from the health care ministry team and pastors were helpful as well as their cards of encouragement and prayers. The impact of that ministry made a lasting impression on us. It made Donna and I motivated to repay the many kindnesses and care that both of us received. Often, those sharing their talents or hobbies can make a lasting difference for others illustrating both service and witness.

Have you ever looked back at teachers who made lasting differences in your life? It could be a third-grade teacher, college professor, Sunday school teacher, Bible study leader, parent or grandparent, scout leader, or a mentor in your workplace. Teachers and class leaders are essential links for our spiritual growth and the realization of our call to serve and witness. Teachers in Christian preschools, vacation Bible school, and Sunday school classes along with youth leaders and camp counselors provide the foundation for spiritual formation for our children and youth. Bible study teachers and class leaders have been a constant source of inspiration on my spiritual journey. Witnessing three members of my first Bible study at Countryside UMC enter the ministry was so powerful. It is exciting to realize that we are discussing and studying the scriptures as our ancestors and church scholars down through the ages.

I have been blessed by so many others in Bible studies and other classes throughout my life. I have learned so much from others sharing their personal insights and witness. In the Topeka Fellowship Men's Bible Study, the insights into scripture from the gentlemen in this interdenominational study are amazing. When I have the responsibility to teach and lead, I am inspired to do additional preparation because of the quality of the discussion. I am always thankful for the teachers in the studies I attend. Those teachers serve us by mentoring, discerning, and witnessing to all of us. I wonder who were the teachers at Madison UMC that inspired so many to go into ministry?

Here is an example of the impact of a discerning teacher who inspired a student to become a lay speaker. The United Methodist Church trains laypersons to preach and serve as lay speakers. John Wesley's mother, Susanna Wesley, encouraged him to utilize congregation members with the gifts for lay preaching despite his initial reservations. The United Methodist Church now calls them lay servants. I have always been inspired by those who were called to this ministry. They provide real-world experiences and an inspiring biblical perspective from the pulpit.

Randall Hodgkinson is a lay servant from First United Methodist Church in Topeka, Kansas. Randall graduated from Arizona State University College of Law. He is an attorney who works as a Kansas Appellate Court public defender and serves as a visiting assistant professor of law at Washburn University School of Law. He is actively involved as a church leader, serving in many ministries, and is active in scouting. Randall has served as a member of the Executive Committee and as treasurer of the Great Plains Board of Ordained Ministry. I have always been impressed with his dedication and commitment to the church. I was thrilled when Randall agreed to have lunch so that I might interview him about his faith journey. When I asked Randall about how he became a lay servant, he shared that it came from attending a *Disciple Bible Study* training created by Bishop Richard Wilke and his wife, Julia. Randall wanted to learn more about the Bible and the church. The teacher, Larry Dye, recognized his gifts for ministry and encouraged him.

Randall enjoys learning more about the scripture and engaging in it before preaching. Randall's lay servant training stresses the Holy Spirit speaking through him. He preaches four to six times annually. It is often in smaller churches where he finds it refreshing to experience the intimacy of seeing everyone involved. Often those churches have limited or no staff. Only dedicated volunteers make those services happen. During lunch, Randall shared that he had been taking seminary courses as his time and finances permit. He is nearly two-thirds done with his coursework. He is now contemplating his own call to ministry, not just listening to the call of others while serving on the Great Plains Board of Ordained Ministry. It will be exciting to see how his call to ministry unfolds. Randall's story reaffirms the vital role of small groups and discerning teachers like Larry Dye in developing a culture of call which flourishes as it identifies those with the gifts for ministry.

During my tenure at the Kansas Bar Association, volunteer recruitment was an essential part of my work, like recruitment for ministry volunteers. Recruiting the busiest attorneys and judges, already actively involved in their communities and churches, who were experts in the various fields of law may seem like a daunting task. Yet I found that they would often say yes with minimal requests and would generously provide appropriate handout materials. The invitation was always personal. I was impressed and learned so much from them.

Working as an association executive of the Kansas Optometric Association (KOA) for more than thirty years, I quickly realized that dedicated volunteers with John Wesley's enthusiasm were essential to achieving the goals of the association. I didn't realize that I had walked into an incredible culture of call beyond any opportunity I could have imagined. We read and hear stories about amazing places to work. This was one of them. The dedicated optometrists that I served have made an amazing impact in their communities and the world. They graciously welcomed me into their family and taught me, tolerated me, and nurtured me. When I made mistakes, they were handled in a constructive way, in which I realized my mistake and learned from it. This is the same way clergy-friendly churches nurture their pastors and each other with large doses of grace. Earlier I mentioned Rev. Rick Saylor's statement that his first church loved him into the ministry as he started his career. I experienced the same thing.

Over time, I was impressed with the dedication of optometrists to their patients through medical mission trips around the world, quietly working with civic clubs (like the Lions Club, Optimists, and Rotary Club) to care for the uninsured in their communities and providing free vision care to help prepare preschoolers for school through the See to Learn® program. I enjoyed working with Dr. Harry Liggett to plan a prayer breakfast for our conventions. He would later become a second-career United Methodist minister. Looking back, the optometrists I served felt like a faithful congregation in many ways. The Kansas Optometric Association Board of Directors was a blessing to work with and demonstrated true dedication to the visual welfare of the public. Like the Madison UMC, I realized that associations and companies can leave a lasting spiritual footprint.

I was always inspired by Dr. Art Queen, who practiced optometry in Lawrence, Kansas. Art had an amazing impact on my life with his view of service to his profession and volunteering on the Kansas Optometric Foundation Board for more than forty years. The foundation gives scholarships to optometry students. He told me, "Every optometrist cannot do everything, but every optometrist can do something." This applies directly to how we should view laity engagement within our congregations by volunteering for something. He spoke to the young optometrists attending our leadership classes with practical insights on how you serve as a member of a profession, how you treat patients and your staff. For example, "I only have simple tastes. I only want the very best for my patients." Or, "I always do the right thing because it's the right thing to do." My favorite: "If you need a helping hand, it's on the end of your arm." But the most insightful comment was "Never, under any circumstances, say a derogatory word to a patient about another optometrist. You will be glad later that you kept your mouth shut." In the context of laity engagement within a congregation, this is essential for effective ministry and teamwork. This advice is an example of the golden rule in the workplace. Obviously, it applies to churches where treating each other with grace prevents unneeded distractions from ministry.

Dr. Queen was among the optometrists who inspired some of his young patients to become optometrists. Today, we continue to see KOA members who inspired ten to twenty patients or students to enter the profession of optometry during their career. This illustrates my vision of a Madison Effect culture of call in our churches with congregational discernment that creates an abundance of pastors, missionaries, pewsters, and lay disciples.

Over the years, I watched amazing volunteers live out the vision of Dr. Franklin Harms, who left a lasting footprint by serving others in need. Dr. Franklin Harms, from Hillsboro, Kansas, wanted to promote missionary eye care in other countries. In 1971, Dr. Harms and other Kansas Optometrists founded an organization called Volunteer Optometric Services to Humanity (VOSH). Initially, they sent teams of optometrists with volunteers to Central and South America and the Caribbean to provide eye care and eyewear. By 1999, Kansas optometrists had served more than eighty thousand patients. Typical mission teams were seven to eight optometrists and twelve to fifteen ancillary members. Usually they took five thousand to six thousand pairs of glasses collected by Kansas Lions Clubs and optometrist offices. Everyone paid their own way to go and serve others around the world. VOSH reminds me of the two missionaries on the wall of the Madison UMC sanctuary. How many seeds did they plant in South America that bloomed into disciples for Jesus Christ?

Today, VOSH has chapters and affiliates in many states and around the world. It has expanded with affiliates in Africa, Canada, Caribbean, Europe, the Philippines, and throughout Central and South America. Sight has been provided to hundreds of thousands around the world and lives changed. Often, volunteers have life-changing experiences and get more out of serving others than those served. This is an amazing benefit of volunteering. This is also affirmed by those volunteering for church ministries as well. For more than twenty years, I am aware of United Methodist Churches providing care and assistance for those children and families living around trash dumps in Mexico to survive. Today this issue is being addressed globally by the Trash Mountain Project which is headquartered in Topeka, Kansas. We now see those children who had been working the trash dumps getting medical care, meals, and an opportunity for an education. The needs are so great, but it is inspiring to see how many churches and Christians are rallying to address this issue and volunteering to help.

Once churches start ministries outside the walls of their churches, it becomes easier to recruit volunteers, building momentum to do more. This also applies to associations and other civic organizations. Today, Kansas has volunteer optometrists who provide eye care to athletes during Special Olympics events. Optical laboratories cooperate and serve by providing eyewear if needed. There are other charitable care efforts as well. It was overwhelming watching these volunteer efforts multiply. It mirrors the amazing ministry volunteer efforts growing in many churches. There are so many inspiring new church ministries addressing issues today, from human trafficking and various addictions to bullying and immigration, to name a few.

After reflecting on forty years working with volunteers and serving as a church volunteer, let me share some guidelines for effective use of volunteers. Each guideline provides a lesson that has a direct correlation to developing ministry volunteers and demonstrating a culture of call, which applies to the church and the world beyond its doors.

First, laity engagement starts with congregational discernment, just as we have learned from those who are called to become pastors. All kinds of small groups provide volunteer discernment opportunities from Sunday school classes, Bible study, mission teams, and prayer groups, along with worship services. Each experience allows perceptive disciples to identify potential volunteers. Generally, churches have a nominating committee. Often, the responsibility of recruiting volunteers is viewed as a burden. With prayerful discernment, it is the opportunity of a lifetime to start the uninvolved on a path that may turn them into a lay disciple, pewster, missionary, or pastor. Churches have opportunities to help and minister to others around them by sending forth those in the pews to serve and make a difference. My goal is to involve as many individuals in the congregation to serve as laity volunteers as possible. No volunteers, or just a few volunteers, means limited ministry and missed opportunities. Serving allows faithful disciples to better understand ministry while allowing them to take ownership of the various ministries as they invite others to join them.

Second, it is surprising how many individuals have never been asked to serve in a church ministry, on a committee, mission team, as a greeter, as an usher once a month, or to help feed the hungry. Never assume someone is too busy or doesn't care. Personal invitations work best. Even asking someone to provide food for the youth group or help deliver food and clothing to those in need can be an eye-opening experience. This small step may start someone on the road to becoming an excellent ministry volunteer. Invitational opportunities to serve is an essential step both in the context of a church, or, in my experiences, as an association executive.

Third, it is vital that those serving on committees or ministry teams have an orientation about their role and responsibility. It isn't hard. It can be as simple as asking them to come thirty minutes early for orientation before their first meeting at the beginning of the year, or have the orientation added to a meeting agenda. Current members may want a refresher as well. Generally, the United Methodist Church asks folks to serve for three-year terms. The goal of the orientation is to have productive members as soon as possible. I also want to avoid hearing the following comment: "I didn't understand how important our committee or mission team was until my third year of service." Encourage questions to clarify the responsibilities of the committee or mission team. There are no silly or dumb questions. Explaining the terminology, process, and procedures used by the committee or mission team for ministry must be included in the orientation. There must be a clear understanding of the mission. It is always good to have a short history and examples of the impact of the ministry provided by that committee or mission team.

Fourth: We will be back! When someone declines to serve, it is important to thank them for considering the opportunity. Nothing in *The United Methodist Book of Discipline* says you can't be persistent. I always reinforce that we believe that all have been gifted to serve and could have a meaningful impact on our future ministry. I go one step further and say we will be asking you to serve again in the future. Please consider where you might want to be of service. I have found that planting the seed for service is important. Someone might not say yes for five to ten years. Patience and graceful persistence will pay dividends. I always interpret no to mean "not yet." It changes your entire attitude toward being invitational to others.

Fifth, always allow flexibility with volunteers to help monthly or quarterly to accommodate their schedule. Regular participation is important if they are serving on committees or mission teams. When regular absences occur, it serves the team if reasons for absences are discovered. Never burn bridges with volunteers. Flexibility means allowing someone to serve with a promise to try it for a year. My goal is to avoid burning out volunteers and always honor requests to step back for a while.

Finally, the most important guideline is regularly thanking and recognizing ministry volunteers, just like we discussed for pastors. Many churches without staff or with limited staff regularly recognize and thank volunteers during services and in newsletters. Rev. Morgan Whittaker Smith mentioned having served in a smaller church where during worship service members would give their thanks and witness to those who cared for them and helped them during an illness. Someone would take a microphone around the church, allowing congregation members to share their joys and concerns. There is one caveat. Never relinquish control of the microphone to those speaking, so the service will end before dark! Pastor Linda Louderback developed a process where people could write joys, concerns, and thanks on a card, which was given to the pastor or a designated layperson to make the announcements. Other churches print the thank-you notes in church bulletins or newsletters. Frankly, the only thing that matters is that we thank those ministering to us.

Never missing an opportunity to share joys and concerns in any format is essential and meaningful. It allows those who were helped to say thank you to someone who served and ministered to them. It is impossible to says thanks enough to those who volunteer in your church, whether they are ushering, providing music, going on mission trips, going to health care facilities, or volunteering for various ministries. Consistent care and training is essential for both pastors and ministry volunteers. When mission teams or committee volunteers end their term of service, it is always vital for the chair and pastor to thank them for their service. It increases the chances that they would be willing to serve in another capacity if asked in the future. Many churches have a quarterly "thanks for serving" meal.

We have now discussed recruitment, training, mentoring, and spiritual care of our ministry volunteers or partners for laity engagement. It is impossible to implement ministry and effectively minister to each other without ministry volunteers or partners. My point is that discerning congregations, like the Madison Church, realize that laity engagement and a culture of volunteering requires prayerful discernment, watchful laity, and even some humor throughout the year. Are you asking the right questions to create meaningful laity engagement?

John Wesley provides the perfect definition of laity engagement in this quote, which inspires all of us. "Do all the good you can. By all the means you can. In all the ways you can. In all the places you can. At all the times you can. To all the people you can. As long as ever you can."

Discernment Questions

- What does volunteering look like in your congregation?
- What examples of sharing leadership opportunities do you recall?
- Discuss possible plans for your congregation to explore creative ways to engage others, mentor them, and train them to be your future congregation leaders.
- Would you consider a ministry fair to educate others about the opportunities to serve? Some congregations prefer to use spiritual gift surveys as a tool to help identify gifts for serving. Is there an approach that works best for your church? If these surveys are used, please be sure to find places for those persons to serve with those gifts!
- Are you regularly updating the congregation on current ministries and thanking them for their ongoing support? What would this look like?

Chapter 6

What Is Your Spiritual Footprint?

Close your eyes and try to imagine what your spiritual footprint looks like. I am always inspired by the lasting spiritual footprints left by the psalmists, Gospel writers, and the New Testament books written by the apostle Paul. They were divinely inspired, which is why they speak to us today. Next, I am drawn to Martin Luther and John Wesley. There are many excellent books and resources about both. In 2017, churches celebrated the 500th Anniversary of Martin Luther posting his ninety-five theses on the Wittenberg Church door. It was October 31, 1517. Martin Luther had an experience in a lightning storm that motivated him to change from the study of law to theology. The result was the Protestant Reformation, which grew out of his works and writings and provided an amazing spiritual footprint.

Recently, I had the opportunity to teach from Reverend Adam Hamilton's book *Revival: Faith as Wesley Lived It*. It is estimated that John Wesley traveled 250,000 miles or more across Great Britain to preach outdoors—on foot, on horseback, and, later in his eighties, by carriage. During his fifty-two years of preaching, he averaged about fifteen sermons a week and over forty thousand sermons in his lifetime. Reverend Hamilton shares in his book, "It was the Spirit's power and Wesley's sheer determination to offer Christ to all who would listen that drove his revival efforts." Some of those who heard answered the call to preach, teach, and minister to others. Through his writings and sermons, he helped train hundreds of ministers, which eventually led to the founding of more than forty thousand churches in the United States alone. He left a lasting spiritual footprint with many memorable quotes and sermons. I am inspired by a rephrased Wesley quote taken from the text of some of his sermons. I repeat this Wesley proclamation because it challenges all of us to do something!

"Do all the good you can. By all the means you can. In all the ways you can. In all the places you can. At all the times you can. To all the people you can. As long as ever you can."

Who modeled an example of a Christian life that inspired or helped you on your faith journey? We think of family members, teachers, pastors, neighbors, church family, and friends. Other times it may have been an act of kindness or words of encouragement by a stranger. It could be someone who started a ministry that helped you in a time of need. As already discussed, it could have been through small groups, especially Bible studies and ministry teams, that we realize how these spiritual footprints provide powerful inspiration for our lives.

At the outset of this book, I mentioned attending a Bible study that sent three members to seminary. We started in Genesis, and seven years later, some of us made it through Revelation! There are so many excellent Bible studies, but I am going to mention one referenced throughout this book. Thirty years ago, Bishop Richard B. Wilke and his wife, Julia, created *The Disciple Bible Study.* This training for Christian leaders has been completed by nearly two million disciples in more than ten thousand congregations and thirty denominations in the United States. Worldwide the number of graduates is more than three million. The *Disciple* series is now available in German, Korean, Spanish, and Chinese. Recently, the Chinese version celebrated its 20th anniversary.

Ideally, *Disciple* is taught with groups of less than twelve. It has four different levels. The first level is thirty-four weeks with weekly reading assignments covering parts of the Old and New Testaments. Each level is an amazing learning experience. I have had the opportunity to help teach *Disciple I* and *Disciple II*. In one class, there were only six of us. We learned so much from each other thanks to the Wilkes' vision. *The Disciple Bible Study* is a life-changing experience that only takes the resource of our time. When Bishop Wilke's son, Rev. Paul Wilke, taught *Disciple I* in Houston, Texas, he always opened by asking everyone about their expectations and goals for the next thirty-four weeks. In one class, a dentist shared that he only had one reason for attending. When he arrives in heaven and meets Jesus Christ, he wants to be able to answer the following question with a yes: "Have you read my book?" Spending time in the scriptures is an important step on our individual faith journeys.

I would submit that spiritual footprints are left everyday by devoted Christians living out the scripture and John Wesley's words. It is through our collective efforts as churches that disciples are created. I see community food pantries and clothing ministries supported by many churches along with shelters for the homeless. We often take these vital ministries for granted. We have a growing number of unchurched individuals and families in our society. There have never been more opportunities in our lifetime to serve and make a difference for others than today. Are you being invitational and inviting friends and neighbors to church by providing a friendly, persistent nudge from time to time? Simply because churches may be located in communities with declining populations doesn't mean that the church isn't needed or that opportunities don't exist for ministry. Some churches in areas with declining populations decry the lack of young families and potential members. Pastors encounter churches ready to give up. They don't realize that there are friends and neighbors around them who haven't met Jesus Christ while others may be hungry or in need of prayer. If we try to live out a culture of call and service, you realize that, with laity engagement, there are many opportunities to serve all around us. Lives will be changed if we listen and pray while answering those subtle nudges from the Holy Spirit.

We must remember that being connected as United Methodists leaves impressive ongoing spiritual footprints whenever churches work together for fruitful ministries. Within the United Methodist tradition, two powerful illustrations inspire us to realize the dramatic impact when churches coordinate their efforts. The United Methodist Women (UMW) address many issues from prison ministries, battered women and children, hunger, poverty, and numerous other needs. Collectively, they accomplish so much in our communities and around the world which may go unnoticed or taken for granted. Whenever they learn about a need, they prayerfully and forcefully address it. Second, the United Methodist Committee on Relief (UMCOR) is one of the first relief agencies in and the last out when hurricanes, earthquakes, and other natural disasters occur. This excerpt from the website says it best:

> UMCOR's work reaches people in more than 80 countries, including the United States. They provide humanitarian relief when war, conflict, or natural disaster disrupt life to such an extent that communities are unable to recover on their own. The mission statement is: Compelled by Christ to be a voice of conscience on behalf of the people called Methodist, UMCOR works globally to alleviate human suffering and advance hope and healing.

United Methodist churches around the world who are donating money, resources, supplies, and emergency kits are leaving a footprint. It is inspiring to see them coordinating and working with the Red Cross and other denominational relief agencies. Serving on a mission team to support these efforts is a life-changing experience.

As I completed my research and interviews for this book, I made another trip to the Madison United Methodist Church. Before I entered, I gave a prayer of thanks for the amazing culture of call to ministry of the Madison UMC and the example it gives us all to follow. Pastor Laura Burnett arranged for Sharon Barnard, Chair of Trustees, to give me a tour and answer my questions. She allowed me to inspect the sixteen photos on the back wall of the sanctuary and gave some family history about those pictured. It was delightful and inspiring! Sharon pointed out that one of the ministers pictured was Dan Horst, who grew up in the Madison Church. Dan Horst now owns and operates a nonprofit church camp in Missouri. It is called

Camp Hebron, a church camp and retreat facility on Lake Pomme de Terre near Pittsburg, Missouri. He and his wife, Janie, are both pastors. The camp is now operated by their family. Camp Hebron is described below in this statement from their website. It is another lasting footprint from the Madison Effect.

> Our desire is to help create and facilitate an environment where people can come to disconnect from their busy schedules, connect with the Lord, restore, revitalize, refocus and just enjoy being together. We are a family operated non-profit corporation. Dan and Janie Horst have been operating the camp since 2012. Lukas and Heather Horst joined them in 2014 followed by Fred and Leah Griffith and their children Ava and Asher in 2015.

The Horst family continues to serve as an inspiration to others as they get involved in ministry. Dan Horst's mother, Bettie Horst, is now eighty-seven and still an active member of the Madison church. Rev. Larry Fry mentioned Bettie Horst as one of the discerning congregation members who inspired him and always provided leadership at the church. Bettie and other Madison congregation members still demonstrate a culture of call by discerning those with the gifts to become pastors.

It is my prayer that our churches provide worship and ministry to connect us to the Lord, allowing us to revitalize and refocus. Driving back to Topeka, I started to wonder how many different churches, along with their youth and families, have been and will be touched by this camp and retreat ministry operated by Dan and Janie Horst's family. It is exciting to imagine. The culture of call and lasting footprints are more numerous than we can ever realize, only God knows.

Before I left, Sharon Barnard reaffirmed the Madison UMC legacy and culture of call with one more dynamic example. The Madison United Methodist Women still seek to identify and financially support those with promise. Seeing excellent speaking skills in a young man, they offered to pay for some of his education. They were disappointed when the young man didn't fill out the paperwork to attend college. However, my heart soared because this example shows the Madison UMC culture of call is alive and well. They are still watching and trying to discern those with the gifts for ministry, planting seeds that may bear fruit. Remember the pastors in the second chapter who resisted the call just like Moses, Jonah, and Paul? The Holy Spirit will still sow fruit from Madison's faithful spirit for years to come.

In closing, I asked Rev. Kent Melcher and Rev. Larry Fry to share some of their reflections from their careers. Hopefully, both will provide some perspective on the challenges and opportunities in ministry. Space prevents sharing everything, but the impact of our pastors who have been inspired through the Madison Effect is evident in Rev. Fry's reflections. Congregations and pewsters need to pray and reflect on what type of spiritual footprint they intend to leave for their families, future congregations, and communities.

Rev. Melcher's Footprint

After seminary, my first appointment was to serve Toronto and Fall River United Methodist Churches in Kansas. The Toronto and Fall River congregations had received seminary students and first appointment pastors several times in the past, so they were well acquainted with the care and support of young pastors.

I helped the churches with deferred maintenance projects including handicapped accessibility. I led adult Bible study courses and confirmation classes for youth. Sadly, I officiated funerals for children on two successive weeks at Toronto and officiated the first of five funerals in my pastorates for murder victims. In worship, I introduced short explanations of the seasons and special days of the church year, the meaning of liturgical colors, and lectionary scripture readings. My family and I also started a tradition of providing special music at an 11:00 p.m. Christmas Eve service. That tradition continued in our family in each of my appointments continuously for seventeen years. My family and I loved those folks and were sad to leave after only three years.

Next, I served at Shawnee Heights UMC just east of Topeka, where the church began a preschool and day care ministry in response to the need of faculty and administrative personnel at Shawnee Heights Middle and High Schools, located across the street from the church. The preschool grew from one class of eight children attending three days a week, to a full five-day program with classes for three-, four-, and five-year-olds, as well as day care before and after school. This included before-school breakfast and after-school snacks. To accommodate the preschool and day care, the church built classrooms and a gymnasium, which were also used for Sunday school and youth activities.

While at Shawnee Heights, I took training to become a teacher of the *Disciple Bible Study* program. Approximately 150 students have studied *Disciple* with me, and I am still teaching *Disciple* in retirement.

After nine years, I was appointed to First UMC in Ottawa, Kansas. The church had completed the Vision 2000 process, which the congregation was ready to implement. It included specific strategies for becoming a more welcoming congregation, assimilation opportunities for new members, a focus on Christian education for all ages, and building improvements. We began with a series of in-home "Coffee with the Pastor" gatherings, at which the congregation had an opportunity to tell why the church had been important to them, what the church was doing well, and what the church could be doing better.

Two years later, a building committee recommended renovations, including an elevator, an improved gathering area near the main sanctuary entrance, and an improved kitchen and fellowship hall. A three-year fundraising campaign supplied all the funds, and the renovations were completed. During that time, a powerful microburst storm destroyed the stained-glass windows and devastated the sanctuary. The congregation decided to rebuild the windows and restore the sanctuary to its original 1903 beauty.

My talents, skills, and gifts matched well with the needs of the Ottawa First congregation, which encouraged me to be visible and involved in the community. I served on the Downtown Development Committee of the Chamber of Commerce, which was successful in getting Ottawa named a "Main Street Community." I was active in raising funds for Habitat for Humanity and helped establish a golf tournament that annually raised a large percentage of the funding needed to build a Habitat home.

Reflecting on my pastoral years, I focused on helping people grow in discipleship through effective worship, Bible study, missional outreach, and active participation in church governance, calling people to use their God-given spiritual gifts. I worked to assimilate new members into the life of the church through involving them in small groups, social activities, and serving on church boards and committees. I sought to involve more adults in Christian education and to create effective discipleship programs for youth.

After seven years in Ottawa, the bishop asked me to serve on the appointive cabinet as Topeka District Superintendent, and after four years I became Area Superintendent for New Church Development, serving in that role for seven years. During my eleven years serving the Kansas Conferences, I focused on strengthening congregational vitality for the express purpose of reaching new persons through the Good News of God's grace and love in Jesus Christ.

I have baptized 233 adults, children, and youth; confirmed 161 youth; performed 111 weddings; and officiated 180 funerals. But I judged my pastoral effectiveness primarily on increasing worship attendance and increasing the number of professing members. Worship attendance and church membership increased in each of the churches I served.

—Rev. Kent Melcher

Rev. Fry's Footprint

Being granted authority by the United Methodist Church to be an ordained elder has brought many privileges and blessings, as well as help to deal with challenges and frustrations. I am so grateful for the love and support of my wife, family, and friends, and for the influence of pastors and laity who guided me along this path. God alone knows the results of my ministry. Persons have allowed me to "walk" with them through tragedies and pain. My role was not to "fix" anything but to point them to God's love in Christ and to connect them to the greater love of church, family, friends, and, occasionally, to another counselor. Four hundred and nineteen families have trusted me with funerals and/or graveside services.

Three hundred and six couples trusted me, along with wedding coordinators and church musicians, to participate in their covenants. I hear from couples' years later grateful for a memorable and meaningful event. A few have even called requesting to renew their vows.

Baptisms for infants, children, youth and adults brought new life in Christ to individuals, families, and churches. In two churches, I was privileged to baptize youth and adults by immersion surrounded by their church families. After a baptism, I walked children or carried infants into the congregation to meet their new family in Christ.

What a joy it is seeing children and youth begin to make the Christian faith their own and to grow in discipleship! To help with this I have led confirmation classes, mission trips, conference camp volunteering, children moments, and vacation Bible school leadership. Scouting has been an interest with the opportunity to teach all four levels of the God and Country program at three churches. Prayers at Eagle Scout ceremonies offered the opportunity to connect with families.

Of all the Bible studies I led, the best were the thirty-four-week *Disciple Bible* studies. Church members find it more difficult to commit to that many weeks, but the results were so meaningful.

Conference leadership responsibilities included helping start and organize the Bishop's Roundup for Hunger and serving on several conference committees. I have mentored five individuals who entered full-time ministry. Three churches completed building expansions during the time I served them.

Community involvement has always been important, as I served on boards of social service agencies. I helped start the Marshall County Agency on Aging. I chaired the Board of Doorstep, Inc. in Topeka and UFM Community Learning Center in Manhattan. I have delivered Meals on Wheels, been a Hospice Volunteer, and organized events honoring Martin Luther King, Jr.

—Rev. Larry Fry

After reading Rev. Fry's comments and reflections, the reader can realize the impact and legacy of the Madison Effect. Sharon Barnard's insights affirm the culture of call within the Madison United Methodist Church. As Rev. Fry pointed out, "Only God alone knows the outcome of my ministry." I strongly believe that Bible studies led by Rev. Fry will yield fruit. This doesn't include the thousands of lives touched from the pulpit and serving others. In my mind, the five pastors mentored by Rev. Fry also assures the continuation of the Madison Effect in addition to those touched by his ministry. Camp Hebron is another ongoing blessing from the Madison Effect.

Even in retirement, both Reverend Melcher and Reverend Fry continue to live out their call to ministry through teaching and serving others. Reverend Melcher continues to teach *Disciple Bible Study*. When I was trying to reach Reverend Fry about the book last spring, he emailed that "Penny and I are currently delivering senior meals from Lawrence to Baldwin City and Eudora. I will respond when we are finished." It is so impressive to see both pastors still living out their call to ministry in retirement. Congregation members and pewsters need to follow their example of service.

The Madison UMC continues to watch and discern those with the gifts for ministry, which is an amazing culture of call. My point is that they continue to seek and nurture those with the gifts for ministry today. They have an expectation that more churches need to embrace. It is an expectation that we will invite and send others into ministry either as pastors, lay church leaders, or volunteers in mission. This is the inspirational legacy of the Madison United Methodist Church that encourages and challenges all of us to follow their example. My dream of an abundance of pastors, ministry volunteers, and missionaries could be realized if more churches actively embraced their inspirational legacy.

Is your church willing to follow the example of the Madison church? What could a culture of call look like in your church? The questions I have posed are designed to provide a starting point for a healthy congregational evaluation and discernment for churches as John Wesley would expect. My prayer is that churches will begin asking right questions that will help each congregation find workable answers and solutions in their own settings. In terms of your congregational culture of call and laity engagement to volunteer, are we trying to leave a larger spiritual footprint in our churches, our communities, and the world each day?

Whether this book is used as a resource for adult education, church visioning or staff training, how to create a robust culture of call is an important dialogue for churches to prayerfully discuss. I am always looking for amazing stories about other churches with an inspired culture of call. I will continue to research and learn how other churches have answered the questions posed in this book. I would also encourage other inspired "pewsters" to joyfully share their insights and lessons learned in ministry outside the walls of their churches by contacting me at themadisoneffectbook@gmail.com to continue this dialogue. Are you willing to help lead your church on the Road to Madison?

About the Author

Gary L. Robbins is a graduate of Southwestern College in Winfield, Kansas, and Wichita State University. For forty years, Robbins has been an active layperson at Countryside United Methodist Church in Topeka, Kansas. He has been appointed to boards with clergy and laity in the Great Plains Conference of the United Methodist Church. He served nine years on the United Methodist Youthville board serving foster children. Currently, he is a member of the Great Plains UMC Board of Ordained Ministry and Friends of Saint Paul School of Theology. Robbins has worked as an association executive for more than forty years, earning the Certified Association Executive (CAE) designation. He shares his experiences mentoring and training volunteers in the nonprofit association world and as a volunteer in the church. He has been recognized as executive of the year by the International Association of Optometric Executives and the Kansas Society of Association Executives. He has an honorary doctorate from the Southern College of Optometry. Recently, he has served as the master of ceremonies for the Kansas Prayer Breakfast.

CPSIA information can be obtained
at www.ICGtesting.com
Printed in the USA
FFHW021917250319
51199563-56684FF